A CHILD OF THE WAR

by the same author

ANNA'S BOOK
THE LION OF PESCARA
DIZZY'S WOMAN

A CHILD OF THE WAR

George MacBeth

JONATHAN CAPE
THIRTY-TWO BEDFORD SQUARE
LONDON

First published 1987
Copyright © 1987 by George MacBeth
Jonathan Cape Ltd, 32 Bedford Square, London WC1B 3EL
Reprinted 1987

British Library Cataloguing in Publication Data

MacBeth, George
A child of the war.
1. MacBeth, George – Biography
2. Poets, English – 20th century – Biography
I. Title
821'.914   PR6063.A13Z/

ISBN 0-224-02436-1

Typeset by Computape (Pickering) Ltd, North Yorkshire
Printed in Great Britain by
St Edmundsbury Press Ltd,
Bury St Edmunds, Suffolk

Contents

Preface

For all its twists and turns this book is the record of an obsession. A boy of nine whose father is killed by a shell, a boy of nineteen whose mother dies of cirrhosis, may be likely to spend his life exorcising grief as guilt. Writing about my parents is still like asking for a minute's silence on Remembrance Day, and this is what makes me, I think, a child of the war. Whatever lightens this memoir is to be taken only as a relieving setting. The point is the lives of those who gave me life.

A CHILD OF THE WAR

The Land-mine

It fell when I was sleeping. In my dream
   It brought the garden to the house
And let it in. I heard no parrot scream
   Or lion roar, but there were flowers
And water flowing where the cellared mouse
Was all before. And air moved as in bowers

Of cedar with a scented breath of smoke
   And fire. I rubbed scales from my eyes
And white with brushed stone in my hair half-woke
   In fear. I saw my father kneel
On glass that scarred the ground. And there were flies
Thick on that water, weeds around his heel

Where he was praying. And I knew that night
   Had cataracted through the wall
And loosed fine doors whose hinges had been tight
   And made each window weep glass tears
That clawed my hands. I climbed through holes. My hall
Where I had lain asleep with stoppered ears

Was all in ruins, planted thick with grime
   Of war. I walked as if in greaves
Through fire, lay down in gutters choked with lime
   And spoke for help. Alas, those birds
That dived in light above me in the leaves
Were birds of prey, and paid no heed to words.

Now I was walking, wearing on my brow
   What moved before through fireless coal
And held my father's head. I touch it now
   And feel my dream go. And no sound
That flying birds can make, or burrowing mole,
Will bring my garden back, or break new ground.

The war is over and the mine has gone
   That filled the air with whinnying fire
And no more nights will I lie waiting on
   Cold metal or cold stone to freeze
Before it comes again. That day of ire,
If it shall come, will find me on my knees.

1

The earliest thing I remember is sitting on a tram. I know I'm very small in this memory, because I have my back against the seat, and my legs are out straight. They don't bend over the edge of the seat, so they must have been very short still.

I seem to be looking into a mirror, but I don't think that's very likely, and it may be simply that in the act of memory I'm already looking at myself. I'm wearing a small cap I see, a kind of beret.

Already the act of creation has started. I can't be sure it really was a tram. I know that we rode in trams, but that was in Sheffield, later on. I'm not even sure that I'm sure about the beret. It may have come from a photograph.

The next thing I remember is pedalling my little car on the day of my third birthday. I'm indoors, at Billingham, in the sitting-room, and my father, in shirt-sleeves and an open waistcoat, is standing watching me.

After this, the sequence becomes more crowded. I have to admit that for many years, when asked what I first remember, I tend to have selected these two events, or pictures, and their authority, if they have any, is undoubtedly tarnished by repetition. I don't imagine that a good psychiatrist would accept them as they stand without some further analysis.

The problem I seem to have is isolating what I actually remember from the sort of thing I like to imagine. This comes, I suppose, from a romantic disposition.

I often see myself as the star in a film of whatever it is that's going on. The cameras roll forward, the director stares down from some nearby tree, and I start to swing my hips a bit more loosely as if to get ready to go for my guns.

When it comes to remembering the past, I tend to see a small boy a bit like Just William surrounded by adult enemies in an alien environment. He gets into scrapes, he lives by his wits, he wins and he loses, but essentially he remains the focus of honour, the talisman by which the dirt of the world is weighed and held to ransom.

This makes for difficulties when some ineradicable recollection of cowardice or bigotry breaks through the mesh of dream and forces a reassessment. Invention is easy, but reality sits oddly beside it.

It becomes very hard to reconcile the real me, with a set of fairly nasty real characteristics, with the imaginary, much more classy me – Little Lord Fauntleroy now, maybe – who has all the childhood virtues, and is universally respected, missed, admired, pampered and imitated.

The choice becomes one between allowing this fairly grotesque hero to take over entirely, and gallop about like Stevie Smith's cat doing good, or to throw away his glamour as something fictitious and try to stick to what I can feel sure really took place.

There doesn't seem to be much in between.

If I stick to what really took place, I have to start with my father. His name was the same as mine. By the time I knew him, his own father was working as a night-watchman, and I remember being taken once to see the old man warming his hands at a brazier. He was wearing a cloth cap.

I think this detail is important. In the years I knew him, I never saw my father wearing a cloth cap. I can't imagine him in one. His look was always that of a gang boss in a stylish hat, often apparently pulled low over his eyes.

I have a photograph in which he's standing surrounded by a group of men at a pit-head. His coat, a double-breasted raincoat, is open and he has a cigarette in his hand, and he looks directly into the camera from under the brim of a Homburg. He looks emphatically middle-class, the boss. At the same time, he has the Humphrey Bogart air of having only just become the boss.

Perhaps he always felt that he was moving, as so many figures of the 1930s did, in a world of menace. You had to look slightly dangerous as well as confident if you were going to survive.

I understand the feeling. I think of it as one of the main

things I've inherited. In fact my childhood was much influ-
enced by the myth of the gangster. I suppose that boys
growing up in a rural environment may have wanted to be
cowboys, or perhaps, if they were bad enough, outlaws or
gunfighters. I grew up wanting to be Al Capone.

I quite admired Jesse James, and I was very impressed by
the scene in a film where he was shot in the back while
standing on a chair to get a book down from a shelf, but this
may have been because he was wearing a waistcoat. I adored
waistcoats. It may also have been because I already had a
premonition of becoming an intellectual, and I liked the idea
that a bad guy could also be a reader.

My favourite heroes, though, were the urban bandits of
American B pictures. When I came home from hospital in
1938 after having my tonsils out, I had sixteen pistols in my
possession, and the one I liked best was a small black
automatic of the kind a gangster might have carried in the
inside pocket of his jacket.

This was before the days of the Magnum. It was the squat,
hidden weapon for which I had a fancy – the sort of gun that
delivered about a hundred reports from a thin red roll of caps
that went crushed and black when the gunpowder had been
ignited.

My black automatic was a present from my father. He
knew where I was going. He knew where he was going
himself, too. He came down from Scotland in 1936 to work
for ICI for £250 a year. That was hardly a fortune, even in
those days, but it must have been quite a lot better than what
he was getting in Shotts.

When I was born, at the height of the Depression in 1932,
he was working in a pit, and he brought his miner's helmet
south when he drove down with his wife and his small son to
Billingham. It probably helped to remind him of harder
times.

We didn't stay long in Billingham. It wasn't much more
than a year and a single trip to the Sunderland Illuminations
before we were moving west into Yorkshire, where my father
had been taken on as a draughtsman by Colliery Engineering
Limited in Sheffield.

Neville Chamberlain came back from Munich with his

piece of paper boasting of peace in our time, and we moved
into a slightly better house on one of the seven Roman hills of
the city I still like to think of as the capital of Derbyshire.

The house my father rented was in Bingham Park Crescent.
The Crescent was built in the early 1920s, on the slopes of a
hill. Further over, the trees were left undisturbed, and became
the oak forest of Bingham Park, where I used to hunt for
acorns. The little houses were built in pairs, shored up against
the gradient, and several had large cellars, with doors on a side
path leading round to the back garden. Ours was one of these.

Actually, the Crescent was really a circus. That's to say it
climbed up and then curled round and came back down again
on the other side, and then put its tail in its mouth, like a snake
bracelet. The so-called Crescent was our half, and the other
side had another name. But they formed, and still do, a single
oval.

If you've seen pictures of the Colosseum in Rome, it was
much the same as that, except that our Colosseum was forced
to a tilt, like the lean of a spinning top. When you came out the
back door of our house from the kitchen, you stood on a
platform above a flight of steps, with a view right across the
shallow bowl. The gardens were back-to-back, and you felt a
bit like a Christian in the arena, if you ever tried to do
anything private out of doors. People across the way, and
higher up, were always looking.

I didn't play in the garden much. I played in the road. There
weren't many cars. My father's Ford 8 was usually the only
one, and he parked farther down. So it was easy to play cricket
with our wooden gate for stumps, and the bowler slinging a
tennis ball from the pavement on the opposite side.

In winter, if there was a fall of snow, the road soon froze to
an icy chute, and we used to hurtle down the middle on
sledges, belly-flat and head-first, using the toes of our wel-
lingtons to steer against the curve, and to brake at the bottom.
I never knew of anyone who hit a car, but several boys would
fail to allow for the camber, and go brow-forward into the
kerb. There was often blood on the snow.

Nobody minded very much. Childhood was violent. I was

carried home once with a cut streaming gore from my forehead and no one sure if I'd been hit in the eye or not. There had been a battle at the top of Bingham Park, and an older boy had thrown a stone. I had to have three stitches.

When I reach up under my hair now, I can still feel the outline of the gash. I look at it in the mirror sometimes. It's white against the pink of the skin, like the lightning flash of the SS.

I feel quite proud of my gash. It's like a blooding-mark, the nearest I'll ever have to a duelling scar. There's another one under my left eyebrow, too, but I got that indoors, from slipping on lino in the hall, and catching my head on the skirting-board. There were only two stitches, and the eyebrow has long since grown back and hidden the wound.

So, apart from the vaccination patch on my arm, I have only one scar you can see.

Boys at Greystones School used to kid me about the hole in my chest, whenever we had to strip for gym. It's like a shallow depression, big enough to support an ashtray in. I don't know how I got it, I suppose it may have been from being born. I might have asked my mother, but I never did.

Instead, I've taken the hollow for granted. It's given me no trouble, apart from occasional mockery, and I was sceptical when a doctor suggested, many years ago, that it might be responsible for the off-beat murmur I have in my heart. When I washed at nights, in my teens, I used to look down and think that I was like a girl, with a space between her breasts.

At the age of seven, I didn't think of girls, or not as girls. The day I fell in love with Marina Marenshaw, after her party, I wanted only to hold her hand, and go for a walk in the park. She had pigtails, and I dreamed of undoing them, like knots in string.

Or did I? I like to think so now, but I suspect even this fairly neutral fantasy was a touch more intimate than anything I really envisaged at the time. I would have been much more likely to skulk up behind her and give the pigtails a sharp tug like a bell-pull.

The love was real, though. Not much has changed in that

department down the years. All the symptoms of infatuation
– the heart beating faster, the jealousy of other people, the
obsessive need to feel close – these were already developed in
a mature form.

Even the name of the object of love was glamorised. I
realised, five years later, when I accidentally bumped into the
girl, now older and pigtail-less, at a hospital appointment for
eye-testing, that her real name was Mary N. Shaw.

I had misheard and romanticised her into someone a little
less ordinary than the girl around the corner. The plain Mary
who sat a few desks away in the classroom and sucked her
pencil over mathematics had been translated into the amazing
Marina who might have hopped through Pacific islands in a
green sarong with Bob Hope and Bing Crosby.

These, of course, were the illusions and points of com-
parison of the experienced man of twelve. Before the war the
only two films I remember having seen were *Snow White and
the Seven Dwarfs*, where the witch nearly frightened me out of
my wits, and an even more horrifying picture with Gordon
Harker called *The Frog*, where a detective was trapped in a
cellar filling with gas, and was seen, to my acute and
abominable sense of shock, to cover his face with a thing like a
giant insect's head, a late-1930s gas-mask.

Very soon this kind of image, and indeed the mask itself,
with its perspex visor, and its close, rubbery odour, would be
as familiar as a winter muffler, or the chlorine of a swimming-
pool. I would carry one to school in a mustard tin every day
for four years.

It seems an ominously appropriate memory of fear, to recall
a man under threat of death from gas. In only a year or two,
when war broke out, it was the terror of gas-bombs more
than any other that affected the people I knew.

No one realised as yet that the seeping horror we dreaded
would never be one the enemy would unleash against either
military or civilian targets, but only in cold-blooded efficiency, and with secret planning, upon a submissive population
of gypsies, homosexuals, Communists and Jews.

None of these categories was much admired or pitied in the
circles I moved in through the later 1930s. In Sheffield the
gypsies were thought to be riff-raff, and in Scotland the Jews

were known to me, through overhearing adult whispers, as the people about to take over Sauchiehall Street.

Neither my Aunt Margaret, who was often heard to express her fears of this, nor my mother, who was her younger and attentive sister, would have felt more shock than many other women of their generation to hear advance notice of the Holocaust.

They had a war on their own doorstep.

Amelia Morton Mary Mann, my mother, was a tall raw-boned woman, with strong arms and a very appealing smile. She was born the youngest of nine children, to a burly, long-moustached antique dealer and a lanky, sweet-natured Lowland heiress.

Two of her brothers died in the First World War. I went to see their names written down in red and gold in a big memorial album in Edinburgh Castle. I have a photograph of one, straight-faced in the uniform of his Highland regiment.

My grandfather was a friend of Logie Baird, and his house was full of early television appliances. He had the first motor car in Hamilton, and the imitators of Landseer lined his stairwell with their dogs and cattle. He died, so I gathered from overhearing the family whispers, without a penny to his name.

My mother had a street of mouldering houses left to her in Hamilton, built in the year of her birth, 1904. My grandfather gave the street her family name. It was May Street, to commemorate his last-born, and so it remains.

It remains, but only just. The last time I saw May Street the top half had been bitten off and pulled down and rebuilt as a block of low flats. But it was still called May Square.

My mother would have liked that. So would my grandfather. Whether or not the staring children playing there with bicycles, or even the old woman I saw with a shopping basket, would have liked to hear who May was, I don't know. I didn't ask.

In earlier days, May Street was a quiet, stone-built slum along two sides of a broad road near my uncle's brick factory. It had some grimly old-fashioned features – outside lavatories, even beds draped with curtains in alcoves off the walls of the kitchens.

The houses were two up and two down, back-to-back with a common yard and a view of the waste land stretching away and up to my grandfather's mansion, Kinburn Lodge. At one time my father's sister, who had married an engine driver, had a house in May Street.

It epitomises the distance between the two families. My father came from a drawer some considerable way below my mother's. He must have clawed his way up the face of the dresser by sheer pride.

He never struck me as a man with a chip on his shoulder. He kept his eyes above him, though. He was always climbing. I think he must have believed that his son would one day be a country gentleman or at least a managing director.

He meant his family to go on rising. My mother, I think, was happier where she was. She must have been used to a lap of some luxury, albeit one where the pinch of need was already starting to put its fingers in.

My father's drive to get on may have proved a strong recommendation to my grandfather in the years of his approaching bankruptcy, when he still had a pretty daughter to get off his hands.

At any rate, the marriage seems to have taken place to moderate approval, to judge from the spread of smiling family faces in the wedding photograph from 1927, where my father stretches his legs in spats, and gives his direct horse's smile, and my grandfather peers out with a friendly scowl from under huge brows, like Kitchener's.

My mother had the long flat figure so much admired in the 1920s, and she dressed in shoes and coats that showed it off. There was a honeymoon with a motor bike and sidecar, and it's clear enough from the snaps they both took what fun it was. Time has turned the prints yellow, the way it stained my father's teeth with nicotine, but the fire of what they felt for each other still burns from the pages whenever I open the album.

2

When war broke out in September 1939 my parents were making an air-raid shelter down in the cellar. There had been an announcement on the wireless about the importance of getting ready for enemy action, and my father, ever cautious and active, had ordered a quantity of sandbags.

It's the sandbags I mainly remember — uncouth, solid things that were too heavy to lift and stubbed your toes if you kicked them. Their job was to smother incendiary bombs.

It was a warm, pleasantly autumnal day. I don't know what I was playing with, but it might very well, at this season, have been a specially baked and hardened conker on a string.

I was always keen on the smashing impacts of shell against shell, the splintering cracks of the interior nuts when my victorious conkers battered their way to victory. I have no memory, though, of the no doubt numerous occasions when they were broken to smithereens.

Apart from the sandbags, my recollection of the day mainly centres on the presence of our next-door neighbours, the Stokes. Our two families were combining forces, and the plan was to share one shelter between the six of us.

The Stokes's daughter, Pat, who was always known by the more affectionate name of Paddy, until she grew up and started eyeing boys and felt that the shorter Pat was more sexy and alluring, was a thin thirteen. She treated me with the kind of offhand cruelty used by my Scottish cousins in Dundee and Hamilton.

I don't blame her. I was probably a nuisance. I was certainly a boringly ignorant small boy of only seven, who liked playing with guns and rubber balls and had no interest in dressing a doll as a nurse or lining a pram with dish-cloths. In other words, I wasn't much fun for a girl on the edge of puberty.

Teddy Stokes, her father, was a man of sixty-three, still running his own business as a 'little mester', although no

longer employing the forty men who were once said to have
been on his payroll in the 1920s. In twelve years' time he
would be down to one, himself, though still hard at work,
and producing cutlery of a kind fit for the Queen.

Mr Stokes dressed like an Edwardian dandy, with a flower
in his buttonhole and highly polished shoes. He had very
expressive long hands, and would indicate his thoughts with
memorable separating movements of them.

He spoke broad Sheffield, as my father spoke broad Scots.
They must have had trouble understanding each other. I
myself at this date found much of what Mr Stokes said
incomprehensible, though frequently highly witty, if not
improper, and illuminating.

There were copies of *Lilliput* and *Men Only* kept in the
house when Mr Stokes was well over seventy, and he used to
make daily visits to a club near Barker's Pool which I always
envisaged as rather like the Victorian Café Royal, with
studded leather seats and women in feather boas.

It may simply be that his neat figure, and slight moustache,
immediately conjured up the notion of some villain, dangerous but irresistible, in a stage melodrama. Certainly, his wife
treated him, albeit rather jokily, as if he was a husband
needing to be kept on a tight leash.

Ethel Stokes was a plump, motherly body, with a large
comfortable face, and she was about twenty-five years
younger than Teddy.

These were our neighbours, and our closest friends, hovering in the wings of my memory of that morning, as we all did
whatever we did by way of preparing our air-raid shelter.

As it happens, it was never used. Preparing it was no more
than a pleasant way of passing a Sunday morning. At least, so
it seemed to me. The war had still to put its teeth in.

Our warlike preparations were not, as it transpired, accompanied by any droning sirens, or growl of enemy aircraft
overhead.

My mother, like many other people, was quite surprised by
the slow start of the war. The threat had been in the offing for
years, and the newspapers, as well as the wireless, had

provided harrowing stories of aerial bombardment. Most
adults believed that the outbreak of hostilities would com-
mence at once, and with bombs, and against civilian targets.

I was too young to know about this. I'd heard the speeches
of Hitler once or twice on the wireless, and I'd noticed how
serious adult faces became when they spoke of Czechoslovakia, but, for all I knew, Czechoslovakia might have been
a new kind of shampoo.

My father had made a business trip to Düsseldorf, and he'd
brought me back a clockwork donkey which, with typical
German efficiency, wagged its ears and waved its tail, every
time a key was put in its ribs and wound four times. I still have
it, and it still goes.

What I didn't fully understand was what else my father
brought back with him, and what he imparted one night, as I
sat eating my toast and pretending not to listen, to my
mother. This was a clear conviction that something very
dangerous was happening in Germany, and that war was
coming.

They want to fight, my father said.

I was neither surprised nor frightened to hear that the
Germans wanted to fight. So did I and my friends, and we
often did. It made life fun. It seemed the way of the world.

There were bad boys everywhere. One I remember is Daniel
Graham. He was a little older, and a lot more violent, than I,
and he lived in Ranby Road. This was in easy walking
distance of the Crescent, no more than four minutes away,
but you crossed a great divide to reach it.

The great divide was the narrow but clear frontier between
the middle-middle and the lower-middle classes. The houses
on our side were all semi-detached, and built since 1920 in
many varieties of what you could call Tudor Revival style.
The houses in which people like Daniel Graham lived were
built earlier, probably in the 1890s, and had mildly Gothic
detailing in their window surrounds and above their doors.

The most significant feature of these despised houses was
that none of them had a door on the street. You entered your
demesne down a narrow, dark, stinking, shared passageway,

which contained a brace of facing doors, one for a house on either side. These were their front entrances.

They had back doors, too, that debouched into grimy, treeless yards, which were graced with freezing outdoor lavatories, furnished with torn-up slices of newspaper in open wooden boxes, and uncertain, jerky overhead plumbing.

My mother didn't like me going to see Daniel Graham. I don't think I did go very often, actually, but one day I was finally forbidden. It was after Daniel had been invited up to play at our house. Perhaps he used some bad language, or failed to butter his scone properly. I don't remember. I only know that he was consigned to the outer darkness, and I didn't see him again.

I now realise that his only fault, in my mother's eyes, was coming from the wrong box. He might have pulled a knife on me, or kicked someone in the stomach. She wouldn't have known. All that she saw, and this was enough, was a boy in a rough pullover, with a shock of red, untidy hair, and a pair of hands with dirty fingernails that were used to holding a fork and knife like a pair of pencils.

So Daniel Graham disappeared from my life, but there were plenty of other boys, many worse. The two whose names stick are John Browning, nicknamed Brown Eggs for having once begrimed himself with his own diarrhoea, and David Nelson, who lived up near the park, in a house with a monkey-puzzle tree in the garden.

John Browning's house was on a corner, and enjoyed a view of two roads. He had longish fair hair, and a rather sullen, pouting expression, perhaps from constipation, or a fear of more diarrhoea. Not surprisingly, both of these diametrically opposed alternatives were a problem when most of us lived on root vegetables and bread, and we were regularly dosed with cod-liver oil capsules from the Glaxo Laboratories.

I always thought of John Browning as a camp-follower, a wet. He was probably a cautious and sensible boy, who has grown into a practical father, and a good citizen. But he didn't fulfil my own foolish ideal of being daring and lawless.

David Nelson did. In fact, he provided — as Dutch Schultz did for 'Lucky' Luciano — a challenge to my own desire for excess. I wanted to go further than David Nelson; as far, if possible, as Daniel Graham.

This wasn't easy. David was a heavy, round-headed boy, with a gang of two. I joined it for a while, and helped them climb trees and scramble for gob-stoppers.

I thus had some opportunity to observe the Nelson style. It was a coarse, bullying affair, and seemed to consist of a good deal of swagger on the way to the sweet shop in the purlieus of Greystones School. It may not have gone much further, normally, than cap-snatching and a lot of elbowing for position.

But there were certainly fights. I even lost one or two, but I didn't lose the last one, which made me the leader of the gang, the day I jumped on David's belly outside the school gates.

Perhaps it was intelligence that helped. I was never all that clever, but David Nelson returns to mind as a duffer. I picked a day when he wasn't feeling well, and I bribed the gang with sweets to trip him up.

Thenceforward, I enjoyed a brief spell as the James Cagney of Greystones, until we moved house. David had gone already by then, drawing apart from the gang through grief and shame.

My father taught me to box. He taught me other skills as well, but this is what I remember best. Fighting was never a simple matter of the Queensberry Rules. Nevertheless, a willingness to put up your fists and give, or take, a bare-knuckled clouting undoubtedly won respect, and may have deterred aggression.

I boxed as a southpaw, with my right out in front, and my left held in reserve for the *coup de grâce*. It was five years before I needed spectacles, and fighting was less frequent, and more deliberate then, so there was never any danger of broken glass or a cut retina.

I realise from my natural stance as a southpaw that I may have inherited a left-handed proclivity, but I don't write left-handed, or try to use tools that way, so it may be a case of nurture rather than nature.

My father wrote and drew with his left hand, and I suspect

the sinister aspect went deep in his being. He probably never thought he was teaching me to box in a way that many people would regard as unconventional.

He believed in encouraging self-defence, and this instruction in the noble art of fisticuffs can be set alongside his anxiety to provide the family with an air-raid shelter on the very first day of the war.

I suspect that he might, in spite of being well over the age for conscription, have volunteered for service in the RAF had it not been for my mother and me. It may have rankled with him that he never got a chance to experience the adventure of action.

He was fourteen years old at the end of the First World War, and he may have been dreaming even then of the day when he would slide the whistle between his teeth and lead a platoon of infantry out across No Man's Land to storm the German wire.

Later, it would surely have been a more mechanised war for which he hankered. His practical skills with motor vehicles would have led him towards the notion of a tank regiment or, as I think I once heard him say, a fighter squadron.

However this may, after all, be my own fantasy. I used to walk to school for four years with the badge of the Spitfire Club — a tiny silver aeroplane believed to have been forged from the fuselages of shot-down Messerschmitts — pinned in my blazer's lapel. I wanted, like all my friends, to grow up and become a fighter pilot.

3

Early in 1940 we moved to a new house. This was so that my father could be near his office, which was just round the corner, in Clarkehouse Road.

The new house was a semi-detached one, like the house we were leaving, but it possessed one advantage, intangible but clear-cut to my mother. It stood in a superior neighbourhood.

There are many superior features in Broomhill. The houses are mostly large Victorian ones, built of stone, and occupied at one time by prosperous merchants or what would now be called upwardly mobile steel people. The University is there, and the Botanical Gardens, and in 1940 there was even a barrage balloon.

To a small boy this balloon was one of the main attractions. It stood, or rather floated, at its mooring-mast, in a plot of cleared waste land, where a fire had razed a substantial mansion to the ground.

The balloon had floppy silver ears, like a huge teddy bear, and its elastic sides would heave and pulse at the dictates of some unseen power, as if it were the prey of extreme, though unexpressed, emotions. I would watch it, fascinated, for hours.

Whatever military potential it may have had seemed entirely subdued in the cuddly plumpness of its distended body. I had fantasies of climbing over the wall and pushing my small face into the comfortable folds of its belly.

This would not have been easy. The balloon was always watched over by a group of uniformed and attentive airmen, who would be doing whatever was required to preserve its equilibrium, and keep it the right size, and the right number of feet above the earth.

These men lived in ramshackle metal huts, hooped and grooved like dustbins, and soon to become better known, and more fearsomely resonant, as Anderson shelters. The huts looked imperfectly earth-bound, and impermanently residential, as perhaps befitted the apartments of men whose duties were to minister to such a fickle and dangerous creature of the air.

I say this from experience. One night in 1942, the balloon broke free from its moorings in a high wind, and rampaged across Broomhill like a rogue elephant, with its wires trailing over slates and tree-tops, until it finally came to rest, as formless as an enormous parachute, somewhere in Ecclesall.

In the course of its passage, remembering perhaps with disfavour my months of rude staring, it decapitated one of our chimney pots, and the severed fire-clay was found in the morning in a hundred pieces amid a bed of fuchsia.

This was the last hurrah of the barrage balloon in Broomhill. The escapee was never replaced with a more trustworthy successor. There were civil actions for damages, and the RAF, canny as all service institutions, had weighed the usefulness – not very great, in my opinion – of the balloon as a shield against low-flying aircraft with its uneconomic and anarchic energies when accidentally sloughing off its restraining cables.

I was sorry to see it go. I turned back to my indoor pets, to my fake-fur spaniel in whom I zipped up my pyjamas every morning, and my phosphorous terrier who glowed all night to keep away the terrors of the dark. His function, after all, was not so very different from that of the barrage balloon, and he never, at least in my watching hours, took off from his glass platform on the chest of drawers and zoomed out through the window to smash a chimney pot.

The day that we left the Crescent, Marina came to say goodbye. In remembering this, and her yellow twisted hair as she stood in the doorway, I realise that there must have been rather more meetings than memory can now recall. There were to be other girls, peppering my celibate childhood with spasmodic beauty, but she was the very first, and perhaps this primacy is what requires an almost symbolic simplicity.

Any content would spoil the essential outline of her significance as she enters the drama of my life in the character of Girl Number One. At any rate, whatever the explanation, there isn't any content, simply the memory of her coming to say goodbye.

The move, too, is uncharacterised by detail. We hadn't, as it happened, all that far to go. Indeed, my father could perfectly easily have walked to work every day from the Crescent. No doubt some increase in responsibility, or some further goal in the graduated ladder of ambition, required that he be, as it were, on call.

This was before the days when people like ourselves had telephones, and so the concept of being almost within calling distance of the human voice at the level of a shout made a certain sort of sense.

I can visualise now how the removal van may have made its journey, but it isn't the route I would have travelled, and later frequently did travel, on foot.

I would have taken the gennel at the bottom of Bingham Park, and run down to Endcliffe Park Road, and then crossed and wound through the trees past the duck-pond to Hunter's Bar, and then panted up Brocco Bank and along beside the railings of the gardens until I reached Southbourne Road.

The tree I was later to call the Catherine Wheel tree, because it always seemed to spin, would be there on my right, and then our own pebble-dashed half of the Wadsworth's old-age investment would spring out from behind its laurels and its short drive on my left.

Mr Wadsworth was a thin, retired accountant, who looked like Dr Goebbels. He walked like a rat, with sharp, nosy movements, and he hated small boys. Almost everything I remember about him involves prohibitions.

Mrs Wadsworth was an invalid. She suffered from some ill-defined form of asthma which made her breathe oddly, and kept her indoors. She long survived her husband.

I suppose that Mr Wadsworth was the absolute type of the small-time, exploitative capitalist. He had evidently pinched and pared to hoard up enough spare money to build this one, dreary, 1920s double-fronted house, one half for himself and his childless wife, the other for a succession of rack-rented lessees like ourselves.

The other day I found a letter Mr Wadsworth wrote to

my mother in 1944, with his apology for putting up her widow's rent. It makes me cringe with rage.

The odd thing is that these insensitive and frankly cruel people were still capable of flashes of kindness. They gave me a fine, collapsible brass telescope.

They gave me, too, the walnut writing-box with the secret, mauve velvet-covered recess in which I keep Mr Wadsworth's letter. It serves to sweeten the pill, like sugar around a bitter almond.

It must have been about this time that I started writing poetry. Self-expression is a curious thing. I remember standing naked one day in the bathroom being dried by my mother and her saying, 'You mustn't let anyone hear you talking like that or they'll think you're swearing.'

I suppose I must have been groping, as I've seen my own small son do, towards an understanding of the language of adults, or perhaps I was simply singing a kind of song, to amuse myself. At any rate, what was coming out was a series of energetic, although evidently unacceptable, expletives.

In a way that's quite a good definition of poetry, or at least of the kind of innovative poetry in which the twentieth century has specialised. I don't suppose that my own first efforts at versifying were quite in this class.

I would already have passed through the stage of great verbal fluency which I recall from my mother's stories, told to admiring neighbours or relatives; of how, when I was younger, I could talk the hind legs off a donkey. At a later and more silent phase of my verbalising career I would lean more towards a morose, Heathcliffian shyness, and find myself completely tongue-tied, except in the presence of boys my own age.

With them I had a private language, rich in hilarious recall of shared experiences, such as a school visit to the hairy-nosed wombat in Weston Park Museum. This never failed to send us all into helpless mirth. I don't know why. I still find the notion of a hairy-nosed wombat rather funny. I met some punk rockers who shared this response a year or two ago, so it may be a recurring obsession.

The verses I began to write, in blunt pencil on faintly ruled paper, have long since disappeared. When I stopped writing poetry at the age of nine, my mother had the poems gathered up into a thin booklet, sewn at the edges with thread. She kept it for many years in her chest of drawers, amid lavender-scented scarves, and cool, smooth pairs of leather gloves.

This ambience implies a rather frou-frou, almost 1890s flavour for the poems, but I suspect they may rather have been vigorous couplets involving animals. A flash keeps coming to me as I write that one was about a cockerel, but it may be that this is a recollection of what someone else, just possibly Louis MacNeice, has to say about an early verse of his own.

Better, I think, to let sleeping verses lie. When I started to write again, at the age of sixteen, and was deep in Blake and Flecker, I asked my mother if she could look out the little booklet for me. I was curious about my origins.

But the poems had gone for ever, no one knew where; sunk like all poems − good or bad − in the bottomless, inexorable oblivion of what Carl Sandburg once called that bucket of ashes, the past.

A pity, I thought. They might have burned once and now be cinders. But better cinders than no bread, as it were. Today I'm not so sure. The absent verses have taken on a special magic of their own. No clumsy reality, or awkward rhyme, or obvious image, could do other than weaken their dreamy impact, sensuous from the void.

Sometime just before or perhaps just after we moved house, my father bought a new car. The Ford 8 had succeeded the motor bike of the honeymoon, so far as I know without any other vehicle intervening. The Standard 9 was a definite step up.

I imagine that my father had even better things in mind, no doubt culminating in an SS Jaguar, with a long bonnet and running boards. He encouraged my own juvenile interest in cars by bringing me home Dinky Toys whenever he went away on a business trip.

The only one I have left is a low sedan, beige-coloured where the paint hasn't worn off, and without wheels. The

Packards and the Lagondas, the Hispano Suizas and the
Daimlers, have all gone, commemorated only in the tattered
cigarette cards I keep in a sealed biscuit tin.

The Standard 9, like all cars of the 1930s, was painted black,
and had brown leather upholstery. You still see a few about.
They have a rounded hump-back, and foreshadow, thus, the
aesthetics of the 1950s. I expect that my father and mother
thought the new car very modern.

It could go surprisingly fast. I remember our record was
sixty-three miles an hour, and, considering my father's
caution, in view of the fact that my mother and I were in the
car at the time, I suspect that it could have done about ten
more. This would have put its top speed not far short of a
British Leyland Mini in 1976.

We made many journeys in this car. I remember trips all
over Derbyshire, to the spa at Buxton and to the caves at
Matlock. I recall visits, too, to remote collieries where I
would be made much of by massive, black-faced men in
overalls. I first drank coffee in a pit canteen, warming my
hands around the tall mug while sitting on a high stool.

My father made a great point of being at ease with men, and
I think he liked his son to be an observer of his lack of
pretension. He liked him, too, perhaps, to be a witness of the
deference shown to his father's power.

These business visits rarely seem to have included my
mother. She preferred to be there on a drive out across the
'Surprise' towards Hathersage, with a picnic, half-way, on
the moors. There are many snaps of the three of us, often
accompanied by unknown friends, or recognisable relations
such as my Aunt Margaret, kneeling or clowning for the
Brownie Box Camera.

My father was a great exhibitionist. It was another aspect of
his Humphrey Bogart side. I have a photograph of him
clutching my mother in his arms, with an expression of mock
horror, on an apparently inaccessible stone ledge in the middle
of a high wall. I still don't know how they got there.

I used to imitate my father's clowning, and also his seriousness. I would sit frowning on the bumper of the car, for
instance, with my legs crossed, and my thumb in an imaginary waistcoat at the shoulder.

My mother is often the restraining influence in these pictures, mysterious in a succession of fur collars, with a mild smile, or a fierce frown. She never seems to have been without a pair of court shoes.

The most frightening trip we made up to the moors was to see the heather fire. It wasn't a bit like the burning stubble I've often watched in Norfolk. It was a great wall of flame, higher than a house, and moving fast along what seemed a calculated line.

We'd heard about the fire from the Stokes, and my father, ever keen on an extreme situation, had immediately packed us into the car to go and observe the damage. On reflection, it can't have been so dangerous as it seemed to me then, with its lusty crackling noise, or my father wouldn't have taken us with him. He'd have gone alone.

That's what he always did, when there was real trouble.

By far the longest, and perhaps the most interesting, trips we made were up to Scotland. There was a little café somewhere on the A1 where they served mounds of hot toast under silver muffin dishes. The mounds were cut up into thin slivers, and moist with butter, and I always wanted us to stop there for afternoon tea. We usually did.

Usually, of course, may only have meant a small handful of times. I recollect an Easter and a Christmas as well as a summer visit most years, but I may be exaggerating.

One journey was certainly broken at the Three Tuns Inn in Durham, where my father was staying on expenses while visiting a colliery. For some reason I always confused the Three Tuns Inn with Dobie's Four Square tobacco, and hence imagine, now, a haze of smoke and a rich aroma of cigars in those quiet rooms.

At the Scottish border there would always be some appropriate crossing ritual. We would stop the car and have a picnic, or simply all brace our shoulders and agree that we felt the better for being in our own country.

Our destination was always Hamilton, although we would make side trips to Edinburgh, and even to Dundee, where my mother had a brother. Where we stayed never varied. It was always at Kinburn Lodge with my grandmother.

My grandfather had died while I was a baby, and I have no recollection of him in person. My Aunt Margaret, though, on a later occasion when my photograph appeared on the front page of the *Scotsman*, in consequence of a book that had been seized by the police in Morningside, and I was threatened with prosecution, alleged that I looked exactly like him.

To judge from his unkempt, sea-elephant's moustache, and his rounded walrus shoulders, this doesn't sound much of a recommendation. Actually my grandfather seems by all accounts to have been quite an ocean monster of a character. One of my cousins says that he had a French chauffeur. Another cousin, more romantic, says he had several. Both agree that my grandmother found them too expensive and sent them (or him) back to France.

There are other stories of my grandmother's parsimony. The one I like best is of her taking out the ten-shilling note my grandfather had put in the plate at church and replacing it with a sixpence. These tales hint at the extravagance that must have preceded the final slide into the much whispered-over 'failure'.

Failure in Scotland never means not passing an exam, or having trouble with your heart. It means losing all your money, a much more calamitous outcome, and one to be avoided at all costs.

Thus did my grandfather fail, though evidently not without enjoying a fairly spectacular run for his outlay. I wish very much that I'd met him. He sounds like a man after my own heart.

Apparently his last years were absorbed in spiritualism, like those of that other eccentric Scotsman, Conan Doyle, and so he may well be champing at the bit over there waiting for someone to renew his interest in the subject. I like to think so, although I feel reluctant to sit down around a Ouija board and put the matter to the test.

At the Crescent I had kept my toys in my bedroom, upstairs. Now I had a special, extra storage space in the kitchen, a good-sized built-in cupboard with double wooden doors, and a shelf that broke it up into two convenient levels.

The one disadvantage was that you had to move a chair from beside the kitchen table before you could open the right-hand door, but this never bothered me much. I developed great skill at reaching round from the left and making do with only one door open.

To the left, above me, as I sorted through my belongings, I had the kitchen sink, and my mother at work washing dishes, or peeling potatoes. To my right I had the useful wooden surface of the kitchen table, on which, if it wasn't set for breakfast or tea, I could arrange lead soldiers, or empty out cigarette cards.

My father was a heavy smoker – about forty a day, at this time – and I thus acquired a regular supply of cards, mostly Player's, although there were occasional larger ones from Kensitas. I got a full Coronation set in 1937, and an album to stick them into. I still have it, as well as the coronation mug that all school children were given. Most of us from that generation have two, one for Edward VIII and one for George VI.

When the Queen Mother came to Sheffield on her round-Britain tour after the Coronation, I was pushed forward near to her, frantically waving a Union Jack, and the family story is that she smiled at me. I expect that she smiled at everyone. I admire her for that.

Later on, my awareness of the Royal Family, except through photographs of them with dogs in magazines, would mainly consist of sharing the agony that grown-ups felt in wondering whether the King would ever be able to overcome his stammer on certain words in his Christmas broadcasts.

Apart from cigarette cards, which I kept in an oatcake tin, I had an army of lead soldiers, and cowboys, and American Indians, and even some pigs and cows, less precious these, which I kept in a biscuit tin shaped like a country cottage.

There had once been a cardboard fort, with a drawbridge, and a tower and battlements, but this was vulnerable to tearing and soon succumbed, rather inappropriately for such powerful defensive work, to the knockabout routines of the cupboard.

Everything was just slung in and lugged out, and some extra special belongings, presents from my grandmother, including a set of exquisite tortoiseshell musical instruments, were as badly treated as the cheapest wind-up machines.

I had a little robin that nodded and pecked, and, to my amazement, still nods and pecks, after many decades of the most brutal battering. They don't make them as tough as that any more.

The soldiers, too, whose lead heads were easily beaten off, would have them restored, if they didn't roll away and get lost, by impalement on a matchstick. My sixteen guns, including the free potato one that had come with the first issue of the *Beano*, had pride of place on the shelf.

Thus I soon arranged, and felt happy with, what I like to think of as my stock of munitions. Outside, beyond my little world, the phoney war was still raging with its now familiar lack of event. At this period more civilians were being killed in the black-out through lack of lights on cars, than soldiers in the armed forces through enemy action. But I knew nothing of the war itself.

That was to change, and sooner than anyone expected. In the meantime, I went to school.

4

King Edward VII School had once been Wesley College. It was an establishment of some antiquity, and indeed of some pretension. At the date I began attending classes there it boasted a junior as well as a senior branch, and both were fee-paying.

The school, and particularly its reactionary and rather splendid Victorian headmaster, Dr Barton − known because of his initials as 'arse-wiper' − was very proud of its direct-grant status, and this was bitterly, albeit unsuccessfully, defended against the attempt by the local council to absorb the school into the public structure of Sheffield education.

I remember meetings, proclamations, lists of names, and even speaking myself, at an Old Boys' Dinner, on the evils of people being taught for nothing. But that was much later, and all to no avail.

In 1940, the school was still quite safely private. There were boarders, who were put up in Toby Savile's house at the bottom of our road, and a larger number of day boys, like myself, who walked in every day from their own homes.

A fair amount of jostling and pummelling would take place on these brief journeys, and it must have been in the course of one such bout that I discovered that my class-mate, Ian Martin, lived round the corner in the next road.

Ian was always a frivolous, mocking boy. He grew up into a fine footballer, and a bit of a rake and a wastrel, but he never lost his outrageous and dirty sense of humour. This was complemented, from an early age, by a pronounced interest in the facts of life.

I remember us once in the road outside his house, exchanging information about sexual intercourse. I wanted to know how babies were conceived, and he told me, with authority, that it was by putting two tails together.

So we both opened our fly buttons and tried putting the tips of our penises − or knobs, as we called them − end to end.

There was a disappointing lack of connection. Neither of us had seen a woman's organs, or would have known that they contained an opening, even if we had. Nor, indeed, would we have understood how a floppy thing like our knob could be made to worm its way inside and make a baby.

Ian's father was reputed to be a policeman, though I never saw him in his uniform. Ian had a younger brother, too, of great physical beauty, so adults would say. We considered him to look exactly like a girl. He had curly blond hair, and was often crying.

Ian's mother was much younger than mine, and had a grown-up version of the same kind of hair as her younger son. She strikes me in recollection as a rather sexy woman, who sat in front of the fire with her short skirt riding up, showing a lot of thigh.

As I would have been quite incapable of noticing or responding to this at the age of eight, I realise that she must have retained her alluring physique, and the desire to exhibit it for my inspection, for at least another four or five years.

In the meantime Ian and I were friends, a couple rather than a gang. This was the first time that I remember forming such a one-to-one relationship with anyone of the same sex, and it may have heralded a slight advance in the process of growing up.

It may, on the other hand, simply indicate how few suitable boys of my own age there were available for friendship in the immediate neighbourhood of Southbourne Road. My mother still kept her eyes open for any further signs of intrusion from the Daniel Grahams of this world.

She didn't want me dropping down the side of the dresser into the wrong drawer.

Fights, of course, continued, and with a more dedicated fury. The school playground, as it was laughingly known, was in fact an arena for bloody combat.

Most fist fights were brief and violent, soon broken up, and not always leaving a legacy of bitterness. I must have had several sharp bouts with boys who mocked me for being a Scotsman, or simply disliked my voice.

In fact, I have a slightly odd voice, with an inability to pronounce the letter 'r', and this may already have struck acquaintances as peculiar. However, it was my accent which particularly excited comment – I spoke with a Lowland lilt.

Later, no doubt, through tiring of endless fisticuffs, and anxious to become assimilated, I developed a pair of alternative voices, a Sheffield-accented one for school and my friends, and the pre-existing Scottish one for conversations with my parents.

Over the years this involved me in awkward shifts of key and cadence. It was impossibly embarrassing to conduct a three-cornered conversation between, say, my mother and Ian Martin. I had to avoid certain words, and maintain a weird in-between tone which was probably hard for both to understand.

I suppose, though, that I won enough fights to become fairly quickly absorbed into the gang life of 2A. I certainly have no recollection of any bullying or exclusion. To begin with, I was kept back a year, through arriving in the summer term, and, although I deeply resented this, it may have helped to give me a head start with the fresh arrivals in September.

At any rate, I spent a luxurious intellectual year always at the top of the class. My teacher was called Mackay and was a Scotsman himself, although I remember neither a Scottish accent nor any special favours.

Apart from swapping magazines, an unlikely occupation for boys of eight during school hours, I remember little about Mr Mackay's lessons. I have much more vivid recollections of the art room, where we would be made, or allowed, to exercise our creative faculties in clay.

The clay was grey, muddy, moistened stuff that you had to scoop in your fists out of tall bins, where it lay until required in a solid, amorphous mass. I don't know what we ever made with this clay. It simply comes to mind as a sticky, uncoordinated coldness, and a dry and friable coating later, on our unwashed hands.

Hands were, at this age, our special instruments. They were what we bunched, for our fights, into fists. They were what we used to push chipped metal racing cars down the tarmacked slope at the far end of the playground where we used to re-enact the glorious exploits of Raymond Mays on the slanted circuit at Brooklands.

Later, at Gamston, I would watch even more battered, life-size cars grind round the stock-car track. But in 1940 I raced my own car, a model silver Mercedes with a lead weight under the chassis, and I scored a series of victories. Hands rose to gloat, to admonish, and to applaud; but hands were shortly to reach the zenith of their power, and also of their degradation.

The pilling epidemic, so recalled, broke out when I was too young to be involved in it. I suppose that such episodes are common in boys' schools, but I never remember a later one at ours.

Perhaps it was just one of those sudden, unrepeated aberrations that will cause a plague of rats in an isolated cottage, or a flight of lemmings into the sea. At any rate, like a plague, it broke out, it raged, and it came to an end.

I ought to explain what pilling is, or was. It consisted, so far as I observed it, in seizing another boy by the testicles, either from behind or in front, and kneading or squeezing until he writhed in agony or squealed in delight.

Put like this, I can see that it assumes a somewhat squalid lubriciousness, and no doubt there was a marked undertone of homosexual aggression or submission in the contact. But the main tenor of the outbreak seemed to concentrate on a sudden, vindictive stabbing, clenching and wrestling, much more akin to the general rough-and-tumble of playground life, and seemingly closer to fighting than tickling.

However, I'm bound to say in retrospect that I can see how boyish wrestling might also have included an element of genital, or more broadly dispersed sexual, satisfaction.

This all took place before the age at which most of us understood what masturbation was, or would have been able, for that matter, to obtain any evident relief from it. Nevertheless, the outbreak may have represented a specific, rapid acceleration towards the private, lavatory pleasures of our early teens, albeit expressed here in the more public environment of corridor and classroom.

One boy would be seen making a swift, lunging dive for some unsuspecting victim's fly buttons as he walked quietly along the pavement. Another boy would be found wriggling in someone's lap, with his hands desperately trying to remove squirming fingers from under his underpants.

Most remarkable of all, long crocodiles of boys, bunched up in contorted knots of articulated wrenching, would lie lashing to and fro like enormous human pythons, reducing the floor of the gym to a snake-pit.

No wonder the masters were shocked and outraged. Speedy action was taken, and the habit was immediately forbidden, though with little effect, as far as I remember, until Dr Barton came down to the Junior School in person and, magnificent and fearsome in pin-stripe and shining collar, outlawed and condemned what he called 'this abominable practice', upon pain of the direst penalties.

These included, I believe, several expulsions, and in time, by dint of caning, exhortation, and perhaps a change in the weather, the pilling epidemic simmered down, and eventually died out.

Looking back, it still strikes me as one of the oddest occurrences of my childhood. No trousers were pulled down. No regular partners seem to have been adopted. No emissions of semen were known. No masters were caught involving themselves.

It was a form of fornication in a void – a dry run, so to speak, for the wet dreams of our coming adolescence.

Caning, of course, was commonplace, but not until a later date. At this age we could only be beaten on the buttocks with a gym slipper, and not until after school, and then only by the Junior School headmaster, Mr Baker.

This allowed the expectation to outweigh the punishment itself in horror, and many a boy must have gone along the short corridor to the Baker sanctum with his flesh already tingling.

Three strokes was usual, although a maximum of four could be administered. You bent over the back of a chair, and the whacks would resound in the ears of any waiting listeners, and raise a dust in the eyes of any waiting observers.

I know that adult salaciousness is liable to assume that the beating of small boys is always a matter for perverse delight to the schoolmaster, and of corrupting stimulus to the boy. I seriously doubt this.

The men who beat me as a boy I remember as expressing no passion other than anger, and I certainly recall no sensation other than an unadulterated stinging. It would certainly arouse pride in one's own power to withstand pain without crying out, and this, perhaps, is an evil thing.

What it would not do is arouse any sense of attraction towards the brutal wielder of the shoe. Like the rest of my friends, I regarded Mr Baker with a mixture of hatred, fear and resentment.

His least liked feature was a sharply sarcastic wit, which he applied to any boy who was bad at mathematics, the subject in which he specialised. This category always included me, and I was often the butt for his tongue.

The other teachers in the Junior School included a sprinkling of women, recruited as the men were called up and went away to war. The first I remember was a handsome girl alleged to be going out with members of the Sixth Form. Perhaps she was, because she didn't last long.

A much more enduring fixture was the Latin mistress, Jean Knight, who wore a dark lapelled jacket like a man's and a square-cut skirt over sensible shoes. She had her hair cut short like a boy's, and her no-nonsense brand of toughness went down well.

I suppose that Miss Knight might have seemed a bizarre figure to some of those who saw her, and the assumption could have been that she was working in a boy's school to provide herself with a mannish aura. But those were self-involved days for us embryo Latin scholars, and we never bothered much about such things. A teacher was a teacher and, so long as she maintained a firm hand, and knew her own mind, and kept her temper, as Jean Knight did, she could wear, as far as we were concerned, whatever she liked.

I learned a lot of Latin from her, and in due course

complemented it with a measure of Greek and was able to enter an Oxford college equipped with the right to wear a scholar's gown and draw a hundred pounds a year towards the cost of my education.

5

One of the social benefits of our move seems to have been an involvement with what my mother always thought of as the Scottish church. This was, to give it its full name, the Presbyterian Church of St Andrew's, and it reared its lanky stone spire a mere fifteen minutes' walking distance away from our house down Glossop Road.

I don't think my father ever attended a service there, which perhaps explains why I never recall going by car. There were other men from his office who did attend, including a Mr Chalmers and his wife and their daughter, Dorothy.

Dorothy, at a later date, was to become a sort of godsister of mine, and I believe that I was thought very good at looking after her. This was a knack I exhibited, to some profit, with other children, once being given a 1936 edition of *Jane's All the World's Aircraft* as the price for my solicitude.

The vicar at St Andrew's was a tall, bony Irishman with a very attractive young wife, who was later to catch my admiring eye and distract me from communion. Like Ian Martin's mother, she was evidently able to retain an attractiveness for a young boy over a span of years.

In 1940, my immature eye was more drawn to the buxom charm of one Bunty Colquhoun, a squat blonde whom I got to know at Sunday School. I don't imagine that 'got to know' means any more than decided to sit beside, or perhaps — dizzy heights — once or twice was brave enough to talk to. It will certainly not have included held the hand of, or even walked home with.

Of the other acquaintances I made at Sunday School I recall only one poor lad who suffered from tuberculosis, and wanted to be a racing driver. My mother, when told of this ambition, shook her head sadly, and explained that he was unlikely to live long anyway. The intrinsic romance of the world of Raymond Mays was not something that appealed to her.

Leaning forward as we did, head in hand (since kneeling was thought of as a vulgar Anglican aberration), we prayed for the war to end soon, and for our Scottish relations to be kept in good health. We listened to the passion of the sermons, too, with a careful attention.

I don't think either my mother or I sang much. I was certainly never a singer; indeed, at school I was thought bad enough to be put in a tuneless group called the grumphs, and my mother considered it rather unladylike to sound out the hymns too loudly in public.

Not so at home, where she would thump the piano and unbend into popular song with gusto.

The back garden at Southbourne Road was already well developed when we arrived. From my mother's bedroom window, seated at the Singer sewing-machine which stood in the alcove, it was possible to look down and admire the formal outline of the layout.

This had once involved a central ring of beds around a marble statue of some Greek lady letting slip her clothing on to a cylindrical drum. It has often amazed me, in looking back, that a couple as strait-laced as the Wadsworths should ever have tolerated this near-naked extravagance only a few feet from their dining-room.

What Mr Wadsworth had done was to divide this formal garden, surviving from an epoch when a larger, single mansion stood on the site of our semi-detached couple, so that the more extensive segment, including the statue, was on his side and the smaller, inferior segment on ours. He had also retained the privilege of passing along the bottom of our garden, behind a wooden hut where tools were kept, into an extensive vegetable and fruit area, which stretched away to our left.

In effect, this meant that we were sandwiched between Wadsworth land, and thus Wadsworth attention, on either side. I paid dearly for this in sharply phrased objections whenever I let a ball go over the fence and climbed into their half to retrieve it. The short lawn which stretched from the path in front of the house to the first flower-bed was much too small for any very elaborate ball game anyway and, as at the Crescent, I usually played in the road.

Later on, I would admire the pattern of the beds, retreating in perfect parallels towards the big, stone houses beyond the trees at the end of the garden, but at this age I simply found the absence of rough areas in which to play rather boring.

We had spreads of hydrangea that bleached from pink and blue to a vapid white in autumn, and a clump of spiraea that was taller than I was, and, further down, sprouts of anarchic rhubarb which harboured loathsome slugs.

My mother would make a tasty rhubarb pie out of the crisp stalks, and I was always struck by how soft these rigid stems would become when cooked up in a crust and eaten with cream. I believe that rhubarb stems are supposed to be very bad for you if eaten raw, but I well remember chewing numbers of them dipped in sugar. So far, I seem to be none the worse.

I may, in fact, have been chewing a rhubarb stem when my mother found me in the garden one day and said that my father had had a rise, and was going to be earning £750 a year from now on. This struck me as a gigantic sum, and seemed the prelude to untold luxury in the offing.

My mother was pleased. A thousand a year in those days was always regarded as the door to riches, the magical threshold you had to cross before you were well off. My father was already within striking distance of this.

The war now began in earnest. This was the autumn of the Battle of Britain, and later of the bombing of the English cities. The first of these events made little direct impact on my day-to-day life. I was too young to be excited by the ominous and then exhilarating accounts on the wireless and in the newspapers of how many German aeroplanes had been shot down by our fighter pilots.

My fascination with their exploits came later. We had rationing to contend with, and some weeks of Home Service, when lessons were conducted in private houses as a protection, soon abandoned as impractical, against the threat of daytime air raids.

In fact, there never were any daytime air raids, despite the endless precautions taken against them. It was in the cold of October, and after the fall of darkness, that the German bombers began to patrol over England.

Sometimes I would hear them, or think I did, on the brink of going to sleep. Often, I was wrong. What I would really hear first, if there was to be a raid, or a warning, was the sound of the sirens.

I don't think any child who survived the Second World War could ever again hear that awesome rising and falling sound without experiencing a chill of fear. As with all wartime sources of terror, it was joked away as moaning Minnie, but moaning Minnie was a dark lady like the witch in *Snow White*, who dragged me half-awake out of a warm bed, and had me carried downstairs night after night to lie on a cold floor and listen to a remote, frightening droning interspersed with the dull, repeated thud of anti-aircraft guns.

In the morning, I would walk along Clarkehouse Road with my eyes glued to the pavement for shrapnel. It became the fashion to make a collection of this, and there were few days when I came home without a pocketful of jagged, rusting bits, like the unintelligible pieces from a scattered jigsaw of pain and violence.

Of course we didn't see them as this at the time. They were simply free toys from the sky, as available and as interesting as the horse chestnuts in the Botanical Gardens, or the nippled acorns in Melbourne Avenue.

It must have been about this time that the British Restaurants were opening, with their austerity jam roll and meat balls; and our own meals were beginning to rely rather more on rissoles and home-made apple sponge. But my mother was always a good manager, and I have no sense of any sudden period of shortage or of going hungry.

Sweets were the great loss. There was no longer an everlasting, teeth-spoiling fountain of sherbet and liquorice, or of Boy Blue cream whirls, or of Cadbury's Caramello. Sweets were hard to come by, and then limited to a fixed ration.

One of the worst casualties was chocolate. The traditional division into milk and plain disappeared, and an awful intervening variety known as Ration Chocolate was born, issued in semi-transparent grease-proof wrappers, and about as appetising as cardboard. In spite of a lifelong sweet tooth, I could never eat it.

They say that Sheffield was blitzed twice in December 1940. The first night the Germans had come to bomb the steel-works, but they mistook the main shopping street, the Moor, for that other dead straight street on the way to Rotherham which should have been their target. So the centre of the city was badly hit.

Three days later the bombers came back and attacked the steel-works. In later years this has struck me both as a mark of German efficiency and as proof that their first intention was not to attack a civilian target.

However, this was too late to matter much to me. On the Thursday night when the city was bombed we had had a warning from the sirens in good time, and my mother and father had wakened me and taken me down to the hall, which we regarded, rightly or wrongly, as the safest part of the house.

There was no cellar to the house at Southbourne Road, and the long period of freedom from air raids had convinced my father that no underground provision against attack would be necessary. So what we did was to group ourselves in the corner of the entrance hall opposite the stairs, in a space between the kitchen and the dining-room doors. This meant that, with the doors shut, we were well away from any windows, and some distance from the potential collapse of any outside wall.

On this particular night we were wrapped up in clothes and blankets. I must have been very tired, because I dropped off to sleep almost immediately. The next thing I remember is waking up and thinking that my head was itchy. My hair seemed to be full of dust.

I was cold, and I could feel a wind blowing in through the front door, which had no glass in it. The glass lay all over the floor of the hall, a scatter of brightly coloured art nouveau panels. My father was on his feet, making a crunching sound on the glass, and my mother was lifting me up to make sure I was all right.

I hadn't heard the explosion, or felt the blast. The bomb was in fact a land-mine, of the sort that fell slowly in a parachute and exploded not on contact, but some minutes later, by a time device. It had landed at the end of our garden, and completely destroyed a large stone house about fifty yards away.

The blast had swept through some trees, across our garden, and hit the house at the rear, smashing all the windows, tearing doors off their hinges, and flinging shrubs and flowers into all the rooms. Then, by some curious trick of its own, it had turned and blown out all the windows at the front of the house.

When it was apparent that none of us was hurt, my father knelt down on the glass under the stairs. I was amazed to hear that he was saying a prayer of thanks for our safety.

Nothing else then or since has done more to convince me of how serious the explosion must have been. My father never presented himself as a believer in God, and it was entirely out of character for him to show any public emotion, or make any form of ritual gesture.

After the prayer he stood up and made sure my mother and I were warmly wrapped up. Then he opened the door of the sitting-room – I suppose because the front door in the hall must have been blocked – and helped us over the wreckage of the furniture.

The windows were all blown out, and there was jagged glass in the larger, lower panes. My father helped me through one of these, taking care that I shouldn't get cut.

I noticed that he was carrying something. At first I didn't recognise what it was, and then I saw that it was his miner's safety helmet. He put it on my head. It was much too big, but the straps could be adjusted, and he did his best to make it fit.

Then we all started walking up the road. Once, there was the drone of a bomber, and we all lay down in the gutter, but no bombs fell, and we soon got up and walked on. There was no one else about, and it was very dark.

My father garaged his car about ten minutes' walk away, and his idea was to take us all there, get the car, and drive out into the country, where his boss at Colliery Engineering, Mr Laurie, had a house. He thought that the Lauries would take us in, and we would be safe.

At this time the air raid was still in progress, and for all we knew, the worst was still to come. So we started to walk on up the road, and through Melbourne Avenue, as fast as we could.

This quiet tree-lined walk was later to become notorious as the place where the Yorkshire Ripper was arrested, but at this date such a sleazy association was unthinkable. It was noted only for the Girls' High School and a number of distinguished stone-built houses.

To the right, as we walked, we could see a wall of bright flame. My father, looking over, speculated that the fire might be at his office, and wondered what he ought to do. Later when we were safe he went back on his own to check, but as it turned out, the office had not been hit.

So we reached the garage, and got the Standard out, and my father drove us to the Lauries'. They were up, and shocked to hear of our disaster, and immediately took us in.

It was only the following day when I combed my hair that my mother told me the itchy dust I had first noticed in it was crumbled stone.

Many years later, when my horoscope was cast, the astrologer indicated that I might one day be under threat from some falling body, possibly a landslide or a fall of rock. Then, upon recalculating the evidence, she suggested, without knowing of the land-mine, that this danger might have menaced me in the past, and proposed a date in the early 1940s.

I wonder if some particle of that shivered stone was still trembling, after all those years, at the roots of my hair. Something, at any rate, whether star or souvenir, or simply the transmitted echoes of an unconscious telepathy, conveyed and preserved the trauma.

The Shell

Since the shell came and took you in its arms
  Whose body was fine bone
That walked in light beside a place of flowers,
  Why should your son
Years after the eclipse of those alarms
  Perplex this bitten stone
For some spent issue of the sea? Not one
Blue drop of drying blood I could call ours

In all that ocean that you were remains
  To move again. I come
Through darkness from a distance to your tomb
  And feel the swell
Where a dark flood goes headlong to the drains.
  I hear black hailstones drum
Like cold slugs on your skin. There is no bell
To tell what drowned king founders. Violets bloom

When someone died. I dream that overhead
  I hear a bomber drone
And feel again stiff pumping of slow guns
  Then the All Clear's
Voice break, and the long summing of the dead
  Below the siren's moan
Subdue the salt flood of all blood and tears
To a prolonged strained weeping sound that stuns.

I turn in anger. By whatever stars
  Clear out of drifting rack
This winter evening I revive my claim
  To what has gone
Beyond your dying fall. Through these cold bars
  I feel your breaking back
And live again your body falling on
That flood of stone where no white Saviour came

On Christian feet to lift you to the verge
  Or swans with wings of fire
Whose necks were arched in mourning. Black as coal
  I turn to go
Out of the graveyard. Headstone shadows merge
  And blur. I see the spire
Lift over corpses. And I sense the flow
Of death like honey to make all things whole.

6

The Lauries had a large, comfortable house, in its own grounds, and I enjoyed the luxury of the few days we stayed there while my father found us somewhere else to live.

There was one son, older than I, whom I remember loaning me Dinky Toy military vehicles. These tractor and trailer affairs in drab khaki were just coming on to the market, and still cost more than the civilian motor cars in my own collection.

Laurie, as he was always known in our family, must have been a Scotsman, to judge from his name, but he was a sort of Edinburgh Scotsman who talked with a cut-glass accent, and whom you could easily have mistaken for an Englishman. It may be, however, that he had a strong feeling of attachment to the land of his birth and that he had taken my father on as a fellow-countryman.

This kind of helping hand was not uncommon in the bleak days of the 1930s, and was surely not to be despised, but there were other kinds of help, less acceptable in retrospect than they seemed at the time.

I always knew my father was a Mason, and that he sometimes went away on his own to certain events and associations connected with this. After his death I inherited a strange certificate in a blue folder, engraved with mysterious signs, and, years later, the father of a boy I knew at school told me that I was a Lewis.

I don't know if I've even spelled it right. The brotherhood of a secret society with special handshakes and a willingness to do its members favours has never caught my attention, or held my interest. It marks another pole in the darker, gaudy side of my father it would take someone of his own age to plumb.

Laurie was a bit of a hero to my father. He was rumoured, as managing director of the firm, to be earning £2,000 a year, a colossal income which allowed foreign travel and a public school education for his boy.

I think my father envisaged a day when he might rise to be Laurie's successor or, at worst, his deputy in the firm. At any rate, he paid Laurie the compliment of a special trust, in taking his wife and son to his boss's home for shelter after the raid.

We soon moved again. My father rented, on a temporary basis, a house at High Storrs, further out than Broomhill, though still within a reasonable drive of his office. There, through a cold winter, we soldiered on.

I would be driven to school in the mornings and picked up and taken back at night. Sometimes I would spend an hour or two in my father's office if he couldn't get away early. In the evenings there was occasional sledging on the steep hills in which Sheffield was always rich, and at nights, time after time, there was the eerie keening of the air-raid siren, and the bundled, sleepy journeys downstairs and out to the Anderson shelter.

Politicians often seem to have given their names to wartime inventions. There was the appalling Woolton pie, which I recall as one of the more ironic concomitants of rationing. Before the war we had had the beautiful Belisha Beacon, named after Sir Leslie Hore-Belisha, which still blinks and winks like a futuristic robot at pedestrian crossings.

Sir John Anderson, the Home Secretary, gave his name to the most widespread form of air-raid shelter, an easily constructed humpbacked shell of corrugated iron, and sandbags, on a brick base. You went down a flight of steps into it, and there was a long low dug-out, partly underground, usually lined with wooden seats, and capable of accommodating twenty people.

At any rate, this variety is the one I remember us sharing at High Storrs. My father was away patrolling the streets, on Home Guard duty, and I recall my mother standing near to the door, worried by claustrophobia and refusing to sit down farther in.

She may have been wiser in this than those who mocked her for it at the time knew. In 1944, over a hundred people in a

London shelter died from silent panic when a bomb fell outside and blocked their exit to the air. Silent panic was simply a way of describing the fact that none of them had any physical symptoms of injury. They had died of terror.

For myself, once I was awake, and not so grumpy, I rather enjoyed these nights in the Anderson shelter. I was made much of by the adults, and taught to play a form of solo whist. This was thought a very grown-up game at home, and would normally have been considered too old for me.

I liked the slippery, greasy feel of the old cards, the dim light as we peered for the suits, and the quiet, thoughtful concentration of the players. Hour after hour would go by huddled in blankets and listening to adult talk and adult jokes.

After the second raid, on the steel works, the Germans dropped no more bombs on Sheffield, but we were, of course, unaware of this at the time. Each night that took us down to the shelter brought an undertone of excitement and fear. There was the frequent sound of shells exploding, since the anti-aircraft gunners found it necessary to fire off plenty of rounds for practice, and to deter raiders on their way elsewhere.

There were searchlights, too, criss-crossing the sky like lighted scissors. But I would see these only when going down the garden, or returning to the house after the All Clear.

It still lifts the heart, the memory of that low, rising, sustained horn-blast, which told us the raiders had gone. Within those bracketing sirens, the rising and falling one for the warning, and the even, unvaried one for the All Clear, much of my night-life that winter was a history of interrupted slumber, broken dreams, and a legacy of subdued terror that haunted me for years, like a kind of shell-shock.

I began to have fears that I would die. I refused to sleep in my bedroom without a night-light, a form of low, safe candle in a paper wrapper that burned in a saucer and cast a dim, benevolent glow around an environment of sinister shadows.

Eventually I agreed to do without this, when I acquired my phosphorous dog with his mysterious aura, like the small round badges many people wore in their buttonholes to see by in the black-out.

When I was ill, and had sometimes to be put in my mother's bedroom, I would stare at the veneer patterns in the walnut wardrobe, inexplicably afraid, as I am still, of the swirling, leonine faces in their grain.

These terrors were intermittent, and often the accompaniment of a passing fever, or a brief bout of influenza or measles. I had all the usual childhood ailments from chickenpox to tonsilitis, and the visit to the hospital to have the offending tonsils removed seems to have resulted in one of my more affirmative identity crises.

I was heard from a distance asserting, to a bored and astonished ward, that I was — GEORGE MANN MACBETH. And then again, and again. I was an awful nuisance, no doubt, in spite of the wash of extroverted geniality which my parents were quick to cast over this misdemeanour.

Who I was, and what lay in store for me, were the troubled wonderings of a brain mostly caught up in its friendships, its violence and its play. But these questions barbed their arrows with the poison of uncertain sleep, and with the remembered sureness of windows emptied of all their glass, and rooms I had known and eaten in reduced to a rubble of tumbled chairs, and carpets messed with torn-up bushes, and massive doors ripped from their hinges and flung askew.

There is an echo of that one night of violence which rumbles down the years, detached in its precise cadence, and yet ultimately assignable to those moments of waking with stone dust in my hair and finding that the world had been shaken up like the coloured pieces inside a kaleidoscope.

It was one thing to go out and fight, and come back to a safe home for tea and treacle scones. It was another to have the very core of safety torn out and thrown away, and shown to be vulnerable like the skin of one's own body. Until that night in December 1940, home had been synonymous with safety. It would never be so again.

Our house turned out to be less badly damaged than anyone had thought, and we were able to get it repaired and return to live there again within six months. I've often wondered what happened to the Wadsworths during this period. I have no recollection of their own experience when the land-mine fell.

Clearly, they did survive, since I find them back in position, and just as tetchy and awkward as before, when I start to recall the years following our return. Perhaps Mr Wadsworth had to pay heavily for the repairs to the house and this burden soured his temper.

It certainly strikes me as interesting, in retrospect, that the building trade was still operating on something like a peace-time footing, with roofers and glaziers free enough from essential war work to rebuild civilian dwellings. My image of the later stages of the war is of everyone in the building trade slaving away on the construction of munitions factories and aircraft hangars.

The garden must have been replanted, and a fence was erected along the brink of the vegetable area, where a pile of rubble remained to denote the former bulk of the large house that had been struck by the bomb. It was never rebuilt and, for all I know, remains a haunting gap until this day.

Further up Southbourne Road several other large houses on our side had been severely damaged, and one or two remained empty for the duration of the war. They became a fruitful demesne for investigation and idle plunder.

We would climb in through shattered basement windows and rampage through desolate, aromatic cellars, thick with cobwebs and piled with the detritus of a life suspended in mid-career: jars of unspent jams, boxes of newspapers, crates of peeling bottles of beer or Tizer.

I remember an earlier occasion from Greystones when a group of older boys herded several of us into just such a desolate cellar as one of these, and lit a fire outside, and wafted the smoke in until we started to choke, and then lashed us with thin strips of rubber as we made a dash for freedom.

These were the familiar traumas of my Greystones childhood. Broomhill was a superior neighbourhood and, outside of school, where violence continued to rage unchecked, my life pursued a more gentle and less hectic tenor.

Apart from Ian Martin, I had older friends who were interested in exploration more than in torture, and my days concluded less frequently in bloodshed or tears. There was one particular day when a very different fluid was the subject of attention.

I was invited, with several others, to witness an older boy tossing off in a garden shed. I remember the expectant, nervous circle as we took our positions to observe the spectacle.

I think the boy must have been inhibited by our attention, since all I recall is the steady, flabby length of his member, flexing and semi-swollen as he threaded it to and fro through his fingers. Nothing, to my memory, was emitted, and I lived for several more years before I grasped exactly what human semen looked like.

7

My father's office returns to mind from this period of my life rather more brightly than the various collieries to which he had previously taken me. His work had involved some step up which led to him being more desk-bound.

In fact, a desk is something I rarely envisage him at. His career had begun as an engineering draughtsman, and at this stage he was engaged in supervisory control over a drawing-office.

This was an airy, light room with a glass roof and a long series of slanting boards holding abstruse plans under large protractors and T-squares. I enjoyed visits to the office because they invariably enabled me to enlarge my stock of graph paper and shiny, sharp pencils.

I disliked the hard H ones, with their stumpy, faint lines. I was fairly tolerant of any softer form of pencil, such as a B or 2B. But my favourites were the middling HBs, which perfectly suited my own pressure in outlining battling tanks or tiny stick figures being sprayed with bullets from aeroplanes.

The office had an annual Christmas entertainment, and one year my father devised a masque with parody characterisations of members of the staff, drawn in blueprint in a free cartoonist's style. The anarchic side of his personality was given ample rein in this kind of activity. Perhaps he hankered after a career as an actor, or a comedian. I sometimes feel this urge myself.

The drawing-office was an extension of the main building, and had been formed from a pair of older stone houses alongside our doctor's surgery. Dr MacIntyre, who was already the resident incumbent, was to play a substantial role in my life in days to come, but at this stage he was approached only for advice about epidemics of the minor childish ailments such as German measles.

Mercifully, I never suffered from the dreaded diphtheria, or even the very threatening scarlet fever. I did my stint of the minor, rashy, pustular diseases, lay in bed for the prescribed number of days, swallowed the prescribed nasty medicine, got up, and was as right as rain.

What my mother and father talked about or did when they were alone together I have no idea. I don't suppose children ever do. Some mornings I would knock on the parental door and ask if I could come into their bed, and I don't remember that I was ever refused.

I would always lie in the middle, anxious, I imagine, to be the central focus of attention. The room was fairly sparsely furnished, but there was a long cheval-mirror on a swing that used to be tilted at such an angle that I could see myself in the glass.

Once or twice, when I was in another room, I could hear my mother and father shouting at each other, and I knew from the later evidence of her response to my own naughtiness that my mother had a quick and violent temper. But voices were never raised in my presence. Perhaps there was a firm rule about that.

Evidence of physical closeness was as hard to come by as evidence of quarrelling. Apart from the various moments of clowning contact immortalised in photographs, my mother and father maintained a great reticence in their public willingness to be seen touching or, extreme of extremes, kissing.

I know that this wasn't universal at this period, since I recall with embarrassment a few years later seeing the father of a friend of mine put his arm round his wife's shoulder while sitting beside her on the sofa watching television. They were a couple well over forty, and their behaviour struck my prudish eye as entirely unsuitable.

My mother and father did sometimes go out together at night, but there was a touch of inhibition about my knowing where they were going. I would be left in the charge of some neighbour or friend and I remember once asking Mrs Stokes, brought over from the Crescent to look after me for a few hours, where my mother and father had gone.

They've gone to visit a sick lady called Ginger Rogers, she told me, with placid invention. I was reasonably happy with this explanation, and would later ask how Mrs Rogers was keeping. I was much older before I realised that my mother and father were having a night out at the cinema.

Up in Scotland my mother and father had a very close pair of friends whom I remember as my Uncle Tom and my Auntie Mattie. The tendency for our social contacts to be confined within the ring of blood relationships may be clearly seen in this desire to want the children to regard even friends as part of the family. It was many years before I realised that my Uncle Tom was neither my mother's nor my father's brother.

I remember Uncle Tom, like my father, as a motor-bike enthusiast. The two couples, newly married, had raced with sidecars round most of the roads of southern Scotland.

There was a daughter, younger than I, whom I remember once lying under the bulbous legs of the dining-room table saying that she loved me. She was the first, though not, I am grateful to say, the last woman who has made this declaration.

I have a seaside snapshot in which the two of us are caught hand in hand, meeting the camera's eye with the seriousness of two well-known film stars, used to being photographed and yet a trifle annoyed at being interfered with in our private lives. I must be about nine at the time, one eye closed against the sun, and immaculate, in what looks like a new school blazer. She is shorter, seven, beskirted, slightly smiling.

Uncle Tom's occupation was never plainly described, but I went with him one day to a locked shop and saw large numbers of carefully docketed objects in boxes and drawers. Many of them were small and valuable, such as watches and rings. I realise now that Uncle Tom was a pawnbroker.

This very useful, and widespread, occupation of the Depression years obviously acquired and retained a certain social stigma. You would have done the job, and done much good by doing it, but hardly wanted your friends to be reminding you that you were doing it.

Other friends who were close to my parents included our next-door neighbours, the Laings, from the mining days at Shotts. Their daughter Marjorie, who is married now to a doctor in the Lake District, wrote to me once out of the blue with a touching, if mildly squalid, story of my own early achievements.

At the age of six, she had asked my mother if she might come in one day and hold the baby. Upon being told that she could, she had put on her best new dress and come round at once.

Unfortunately, either the strangeness of the contact with an unfamiliar female, or some overriding pressure in the growing bladder, led to a sudden and copious discharge of urine. The poor best dress was flooded, and the girl who had wanted to hold the baby retired in tears.

I suppose this must be my earliest documented experience. Nobody else is alive who has offered me a prior one. It perhaps brings out an early lack of concern for female sensibilities on the part of the central character in the anecdote, or so the feminists might say. I hope that this characteristic has been outgrown.

Sometime about this date I abandoned the Wolf Cubs. The scouting movement, like the Hitler Youth and the Girl Guides, was one of those uniformed paramilitary organisations which enjoyed a great vogue in the 1930s. It may have been that the ritual of brotherhood in the life of camp and marching provided some recompense for the bloody antinomies of the picket line and the negotiating table.

At any rate, most of my friends, like myself, were at one period or another enlisted as Wolf Cubs. The Kipling association is now one that I rather approve of, but in the bracing era of Auden and Orwell it would no doubt have struck more progressive parents as irredeemably backward, and even Fascist.

We wore green caps, with braided lines, and were encouraged to compete for badges, which would in time form impressive rows, like the pips of officers or the stripes of sergeants, down the sleeves of our khaki shirts.

I was always bad at practical tasks, and the various activities for which badges might be won were mostly beyond my skill. My arms remained bare of adornment. Worst of all, I couldn't even learn to tie the basic knots, which were the cardinal basis, almost the physical Bible and Koran, of scouting for boys.

I still can't make out the difference between a reef knot and a slip one. So you will see that I was hardly the timber for speedy promotion. I soon tired of scouting. I grew to hate the twisted leather toggle which grasped the scarf at my neck. I was bored by the ugly sweater, and the insipid shirt.

This hatred and boredom shines out from a dreary photograph taken at the gate of 38 Bingham Park Crescent on a day when we'd gone over there for the Stokes to admire me in my uniform.

I don't know whether they did or not. I can't imagine that the elegant Teddy, with his fancy waistcoats and his glass of whisky, would have had much time for the sober and outdoor pursuits of Baden-Powell and his boys.

Drinking whisky, or indeed any kind of alcohol, was not a feature of our own household. It wasn't so much that it was forbidden as that my mother simply regarded it as rather vulgar.

Teddy Stokes was always a tippler. I remember him at a later date with his short glass of Scotch in a veiny fist, and his blue budgerigar, allowed out of its cage for a flutter round the dining-room, perched in tipsy disarray as it nodded in and out of the fascinating liquid like a perpetual-motion toy.

I imagine Teddy, with the phlegmatic Ethel at his shoulder, invited to put in a word of praise for my obviously disliked uniform, and silently winking at me, and lifting his glass of whisky, as in the bar at the Midland Hotel.

At any rate, I had my way. I resigned, and the dog-eared manual, <i>Scouting for Boys</i>, lay untouched in the top of my toy cupboard until, much later, it was taken down and read with laughter for its advice on how to avoid the awful sin of self-abuse.

My lack of manual skill often surprises me. My father was unusually good at working with his hands, and he bequeathed me a variety of well-preserved tools. Many of these have disappeared over the years, but there is still a Cremona toffee box, oblong and battered, containing fine chisels, and a lean hammer, and a folding wooden ruler.

These were only the cruder instruments of my father's skill. He had a fastidiously accurate set of drawing implements, like exotic insects from some foreign jungle, each exactly fitted into its own niched cavity of worn purple velvet in a smooth shagreen case held casually closed with a double folded elastic band.

I have these instruments filed away in a drawer. They challenge me with their precision, and their unused steely gleam. They bring the mark of a long-seated guilt to my cheeks, the flush of an incompetence too far embedded now ever to be dug out, and rooted free, and taught to flower in hands learning to draw straight, or pin the heart of a circle, or calculate the angle of a corner.

My dream has always been to be an architect. I admire the power to design buildings more than any other. It must have been a dream born in my father's drawing-office, and in the awed contemplation of these instruments I was too clumsy to use.

My father did, in fact, design his own house, and I still have the plans for it, though it was never built. It seems, when I unfold them, to have been a modest enough, though no doubt cunningly planned, Elizabethan bungalow. This would have been inevitable in the 1930s, when the giant shadow of Lutyens hung like a warming, although overprotective, wing over the infancy of modern English architecture.

My father was also an inventor, and he had patents, which he was always too short of money to renew, for a collapsible pit prop, and a pulley to move coal. These patents are impressive things, printed on cream paper, and embossed with a red seal. I have them framed on the wall of my study. They seem to offer a challenge, and hint at a power, inherited and long misused, which might still, with luck and proper effort, result in some real achievement.

Such is the typical dream of the Scotsman abroad, the puritanical product of the work ethic, who has never been satisfied, and no doubt never will be, either with the fruits of his own industry, or the rewards of his fortune.

One of the few things I was ever able to make, apart from a cup of tea and a boiled egg, was a tank. I'm not sure who taught me this knack, or when, but I still have it, and will record the process here for posterity.

The necessary ingredients are a cotton reel, a stub of candle, an elastic band, a matchstick, a drawing pin and some kind of hole-boring instrument. A penknife to cut notches in the edge of the reel might also be useful.

The best kind of reel is one with high rims, where the notches can be deep, as this will enable the finished vehicle to climb over quite massive obstacles. But even the notchless tank will perform reasonably well on a flat surface.

First of all, you drill a hole in the stub of candle, which should be no more than half an inch long, preferably a bit shorter. Then you hollow a slight groove along the top side.

Next, you thread the elastic band through the hole and keep it in place with a matchstick lying in the groove. Finally, you thread the band, with the candle stub on top, down through the reel and pin it fast on the bottom with the drawing pin. All that you need to do, to set the tank in motion, is to wind up the elastic band and lay the reel on its edge, with the matchstick touching a surface.

The slip of the wax on the wood of the reel will allow the power of the uncoiling elastic to transfer itself to the shaft of the matchstick, and thence to the surface, making the reel move slowly along.

The movement is uneven but with a certain inexorable quality that may hint at the horror of the Western Front, or the glory of Alamein. I had a whole squadron of these tanks at one time, and I imagine that each could still be made to roll forward today – unless, of course, the rubber has perished.

One or two in some other boy's toybox may have survived the rigours of the post-war period rather better than the Waltzing Matildas that broke the power of Rommel, and sent the English infantry forward under their tin hats over the burning sands to Tobruk and Benghazi.

These were glorious names in my indoctrinated childhood, and the wooden miniatures I learned to power with wax and elastic were the talismanic tributes to a remote heroism of technology.

8

It was early in 1941 that the LDV became the Home Guard. The Local Defence Volunteers, to give them their full name, had been a feature of our family life since their inception.

It was consistent with my father's interest in precautionary measures of all kinds that he should have become involved with such an organisation in its beginnings. I don't recall if there were even uniforms to start with, but our wooden shed in the garden was shortly the repository of paramilitary equipment, notably a quantity of small, triangular, yellow flags.

I've never subsequently grasped exactly what functions these flags served. They were made of a stout linen, sewn neatly at the edges, and kept folded in wooden boxes.

Once or twice I would be taken up to the moors with my father and his platoon and would see these mysterious flags deployed in some mystical pattern on the heather. But its complicated secrets were never revealed to me.

My father had enlisted with the skill, or the enthusiasm, or perhaps simply with the priority, to be promoted rapidly from the ranks to the status of junior officer. I never remember him except with the single pip of a second lieutenant on his shoulder.

The platoon was a mixture of men, fat and thin, tall and short, known and unknown. Some I had met at the office; others, I imagine, were local residents who came together with the rest simply for exercises.

No doubt these were an entertaining way of passing a Saturday afternoon, away from the womenfolk − for there were no female recruits in the LDV − and with the prospect of man's talk about football or politics, and even a glass of beer to end with at some suitable public house.

Whether or not my father indulged in these extra-curricular pursuits I have no idea. He certainly never touched alcohol at home, nor was seen to in my presence out of doors.

All I recall is the flat extent of the moorland, the burned patches in the heather, the men spread out in lines, kneeling or standing, and the positions of the flags being altered at some shouted command, or blast of a whistle. It makes an odd recollection of a military manoeuvre.

The particular area favoured for the exercises was a barren spot known as the Surprise, because, on passing between two rocky bastions, one at either side of the road, the moorland suddenly offered a prospect of a rolling valley on the way down to the village of Hathersage.

With a typical transference of childhood, I always regarded the moorland itself as being the Surprise and not, as it should have been, the inviting view of the valley. The sheer bareness of the moor was a greater source of astonishment than the more populated landscape of the other side.

Nearby, there was a spectacular stone, visible from some considerable distance. This landmark was known as the Toad Rock, and indeed the rusty pitted back of the rock did hint at the warty carapace of some prehistoric and larger-than-life reptilian.

I drove by again many years later, and the Toad Rock was still there, undisturbed in its primeval slumber. But the yellow flags and the men working with them had gone for ever.

One of the conveniences of our house at Southbourne Road was that it stood at an equal distance between two useful shopping centres. The older one, at Hunter's Bar, which we had used from the Crescent, was at the bottom − alas, if you were coming back with a heavy shopping basket − of a steep hill called Brocco Bank.

The names of streets in this part of Sheffield are oddly romantic. I remember once telling John Betjeman that I had been brought up in Broomhill, and his face lighting up with recollected wonder as he began to chant: Hangingwater Road, Hangingwater Road.

Until then, this immensely evocative name had struck me as no more remarkable than Oxford Street or Trafalgar Square. But the interrupted cataract, the pausing torrent in the air, redolent with the scent of Arabian blossoms, as from some wondrous garden in the illustration to a children's book – this is now a permanent feature of my imagination.

Endcliffe Park, too, has taken on an air of substantial mystery which it lacked in 1941. I now wonder when I return to it where the cliff was thought to end, and what happened to the great sea that must formerly have beaten at the rocks of Hunter's Bar.

Endcliffe Park, to me, was simply where I went to catch tiddlers in a jam jar, and sometimes fed the ducks with soggy bread. It was less ominous in its associations than the park at Meadowhead, where I once, at the age of five, nearly drowned in a small pool.

The pool was only three feet deep, and I could easily have saved myself by standing up on the bottom, but this practical resource failed to occur to me as the dirty water flooded into my throat. I had to be fished out with a stick, wallowing like a suicide, and spitting water mixed with vomit.

Later on I would learn to swim, and feel astonished to think that I could nearly have drowned in such a shallow depth of water. But I know now that even a puddle can be enough. It simply depends on the mouth and nostrils being below the surface.

Hunter's Bar lay round a central garden in the middle of a tidy roundabout, and it offered a variety of shops from a paying lending library, patronised by my mother for romance, to a branch of the Yorkshire Penny Bank, with a grand, mulled marble frontage swelling, in ocean liner style, right round a corner.

The shop I remember best is the grocer's, where my mother would place a weekly order. At least, she would do that in the early days of the war. Boys to go on rounds with bicycles were no longer available after the inception of universal conscription.

There used to be open bags in the grocer's with oats and butter-beans, though not, I think, with rice or spaghetti. As a baby I had eaten rice pudding, but I soon developed an aversion for it. Spaghetti I always regarded as just like worms.

The baker's, which stood next door to the grocer's, was a less frequent stopping place, except for ordinary loaves. My mother baked all our tea bread and cakes at home, like most Scottish wives of her generation, and it never occurred to her, or us, to suppose that shop-baked stuff would be of the same quality.

Later, I do remember her buying me Eccles cakes there, and occasionally a fruit pie made with bilberries. I liked the indelible purple stain this made, like the marks of the indelible pencils from my father's office which you had to lick with the tip of your tongue.

Perhaps the purchase of these southern delicacies marked a temporary boredom with the oven on my mother's part, or perhaps they were thought to introduce some minor element of a foreign cuisine into our household fare. I never asked. I enjoyed them, and ate up in silence.

The shopping centre at Broomhill was improved after the blitz by the arrival, evacuated from the city centre for the duration, of a large store called Walsh's. The store was accommodated in what must once have been a distinguished mansion, classical in style, with a pillared frontage, and a pair of Greek pediments.

Entering through the imposing porch, one was rapidly part of a woman's world of dresses on hangers, mirror-topped counters that sold lipstick and cold-cream, and an annexe with potted palms where afternoon tea was served.

Women in the 1940s did a good deal more drinking of morning coffee and afternoon tea than they do now. My Aunt Margaret, a woman who had had to fend for herself since the 1920s, when her doctor husband was carried off by some long-forgotten disease, was prone to hint that a fortune awaited anyone who cared to open a Scottish tea salon in England.

She may have been right. I occasionally fantasise nowadays over fresh-cheeked waitresses in tartan aprons, bringing loaded tiers of morning rolls, oatcakes and mutton pies to the jaded world of some London suburb, satiated with Wimpy bars and fish and chip shops.

Nothing like this was available in Broomhill. Some days we would go into town on the bus, and eat a high tea at

Cole's, or possibly Davey's, which still occupied its old site in Barker's Pool. Davey's was my favourite. They specialised in something I have never eaten before or since, a delicious tomato sausage, which would be fried with vinegar-flavoured chips and served skinless.

These sausages could be bought in half-pounds at Davey's branch shop at Hunter's Bar, and they were a prized feature of Saturday dinners. Dinner, in the north-country fashion, was a meal eaten in the middle, and not as with more hoity-toity southerners at the end, of the day.

Food was always a matter of great concern in the war. Perhaps it always is for children, war or no war. Indeed, it soon distracts any recollecting mind from almost every other memory that arises to compete with it.

So that here, on an imaginary winter's day in February of 1941, my mother and I are pushing our way through a flurry of rain with heads down against the wind, and our arms aching under baskets laden with potatoes and apples, loaves of bread and packets of biscuits, bottles of HP sauce and canisters of Saxa salt.

The supply of provisions became the main duty of we camp-followers. Napoleon was right to say that an army marches on its stomach. And we were, indeed, an army, one equipped with electric torches for walking in the black-out, and with stirrup-pumps to empty water from shelters, and with tin hats for the ARP, and with gas-masks for all our children.

The civilian population had gone to war.

Evacuation, as it was unfortunately called — implying, so it has always seemed to me, the discharge of an unwanted waste product — was already well under way by this time. A few children had been shipped abroad to the United States, and I recall in my very first term at King Edward's the sight of a short, large-headed boy with longish hair standing on the platform of the Junior School Hall and making a farewell speech. He was due to sail on the *Queen Mary* the following day.

I was not to see this boy again for nearly twelve years when, older, besuited, and still noticeably large-headed, he looked round the door of my study at Oxford with a batch of magnificent poems. His name was Anthony Thwaite.

Other boys went to the country. On the whole, though, the Sheffield blitz was felt to mark the end rather than the beginning of a period of great danger for children, and so evacuation was never extensively carried out.

The daily walks to school along streets littered with the detritus of aerial combat, the nightly overhearing of news bulletins grim with the propaganda of retreat, the frequent stoppings of lessons to practise the rapid donning of our respiratory apparatus − these became the ceremonies of a shared world.

The gas-mask practices were particularly involving. It was quite difficult to make the respirator fit snugly both over the hair and under the chin. It tended to catch loose strands under the adjustable straps, or to ease up over the mouth.

Properly fitted, it would still tend to steam over and cloud the eye-piece with a veiling mist, like a window in a hot room after rain. Sounds would clog into a soupy thickness, and the strange, gas-mask smell compounded of stale air, hot rubber and congealed fear would rise like a coiling miasma to block the nose.

This smell sometimes seemed as bad as mustard gas itself. Indeed, the associations of mustard − hot, slimy and yellow, as it seemed to a group of boys too young to have enjoyed a dab of sharp Colman's on rare steak − were a prevalent side-menace in the business of dressing up for a gas attack.

The metal containers for the masks, bleakly inscribed GAS MASKS in harsh black, were themselves painted a violent mustard green. It wasn't hard to think that you could almost taste the awful stuff as you bent your gasping face over the desk.

Still, these grim rituals, like the later filing down into prepared shelters, were a welcome break from the ordinary business of lessons and, as such, were cherished and looked forward to.

One of the odder verbal effects of the war was a great speeding up in the spread of catch-phrases.

Hitler, with his rapid-fire delivery and his repeated slogans, was quick to exploit the commanding potential of the wireless, as was Winston Churchill, with his grand exhortations about fighting on the beaches, and his clapping, so I have been told, of one hand over the microphone and adding, 'And we shall clout them with beer bottles because that's about all we've bloody well got.'

The lead given by these maestros was followed by a host of imitators. The voice of Lord Haw-Haw was heard in the land, as was the guying voice of his parody analogue in Tommy Handley's ITMA: 'Dis iss Fumph speaking.'

Goebbels pioneered the use of propaganda in Nazi Germany, but some of our own manipulators of the airways and the billboards were no slouches either. As a small boy, I seemed to live in a world constantly broken by pithy exhortations and concise warnings, from *Dig for Victory* to *Careless Talk Costs Lives*.

Not all of these were wisely chosen. In particular, the wording of some popular patriotic songs could easily give offence. You didn't go too far wrong with 'Roll out the Barrel' or an Anglicised version of 'Lili Marlene', but you were in real trouble when it came to a song like 'There'll Always Be an England'. I remember hunching down inside my overcoat collar, upstairs on a bus one night in Scotland, when a crowd from the dog track struck up this execrable song with brutal irony. It wouldn't have done for anyone to hear me singing along with the 'Red, white and blue, what can I do for you' in what might have been mistaken, despite my inbred Scottishness, for an English accent.

There were lewd undertones, too, in some of the comedy catch-phrases. I didn't fully grasp the *double entendre* of *Can I do you now, Sir?* the first time I heard it, but by the end of the war 'doing' a woman was standard adolescent slang for sexual intercourse.

Not surprisingly, the little world of King Edward's mimed the larger one of England at war. Certain catch-phrases caught on, and ran the gamut of fascinated approval, bored rejection, and final oblivion. One of the oddest was: *Prove it*.

I don't know what youthful philosopher introduced me to this irritating tag, but I do know how utterly amazing it seemed that you could answer any statement on any subject whatsoever with a truculent challenge.

The phrase wasn't much tried on masters at school, who would have had a swift way with insisters, but it became the bane of home life. The phrase seemed to have a talismanic significance. I would use it with glee, and with ghoulish repetition.

Perhaps this was early evidence of a sceptical disposition, or of a taste for argument. Proving, at any rate, whether it be a proposition, or oneself, has remained a lifelong interest. The inexplicable traumas of the war, together with the physical challenges they offered to the system, may have had more than a little to do with this.

9

Reading is one of the great pleasures of my life. I sometimes think I could manage well enough without writing, but not without books. Exactly when I started reading I'm not sure now, but there must have been some lost, narrow thread between being read to and picking up some pictured volume for myself.

The first origins of the business were probably bedtime stories, invented out of the air, and woven from near-surreal materials to make me go to sleep, halting at some arbitrary point with the arrival of the Sandman, and renewing their dislocated advance the following night.

After these, there will have been those large, square-cut folios which offered printed and thus definitive tellings of the great fairy tales. Beyond the most misty recall of these – Norwegian trolls in dark and sinister forests – I have no memory of who wrote what, or indeed of who read what to me. I suspect that my mother and father took turns.

The first books I do remember were certainly in my own hands, and I think thus that the engrossing primacy of print was borne in on me fairly early on. I started to enjoy what I could physically hold and use as a basis for fantasy at the same time.

I still enjoy the feel of a book, and it seems to me vital that it should have a pleasing surface, a reasonable weight and a nice smell. I don't ever recall as a child actually getting my teeth into a good book, though I was once discovered in the cellar tasting coal – a rather literal way of fuelling the mind.

I evidently latched on to the fact quite early on that a book could supply some kind of sustenance, and some kind of pastime. The content of this must have varied a good deal, since we had few books at home – I write 'few', but I don't recall *any* made available to me – and so what I could get to read came from a children's library.

The stories that appealed most were ones about animals that

talked. These were not the traditional, rather upper-class Beatrix Potter tales. I was a reader intent upon slightly larger blocks of print, and fewer pictures, than these tiny volumes offer.

Forests, and rabbits, jostle vaguely in my consciousness. Then there is a large jump, and I have a totally different sort of publication in my hands: the slender, fluttering, coarse-grained sheets of a series of so-called comics, very notably the *Dandy*, with its opening sagas of Desperate Dan, and its ingenious blend of wordy balloon, sub-text, and graphic, cinematic images.

I'm not sure whether comics appealed because they used the same techniques of story-telling as the cinema, or vice versa, but I feel sure there was a connection. Later, the *Dandy*, and its sister periodical the *Beano*, born in my lifetime, would give way to more hectic and blood-ridden weeklies – my favourite *Hotspur*, with its chronicles of Red Circle School, and the *Wizard*, with its astonishing hero, the great Wilson, who carried something in a silver Crawford's biscuit tin, and could run a mile in three minutes. I am still eagerly waiting, forty years later, for this achievement to be equalled.

There were other comics, the *Rover* and the *Champion*, to name only two, but perhaps my main and enduring fascina-tion, from the age of eight on, for several years, was with the William books. I once boasted of having read the whole series before I was twelve. William the Gangster and William the Dictator fitted my own ambitions.

These red, slightly rugged volumes, with their line draw-ings of a scruffy, appealing boy in a twisted tie and awry school cap, seemed to touch some nerve. They were the nearest I got at this time to an understanding that literature could embed itself in reality as well as float up into the land of dreams. William himself had visions, but the banal circum-stances of his everyday life were not so enormously different from my own.

In the background were more reserved adult volumes, my father's *Ambulance Handbook*, with its gory, frightening illus-trations of bodies receiving artificial respiration and arms being bared for the needle, and my mother's tiny black Bible, with its red-gold edging to the thin tissue pages, and its overflapping, dog's-ear leather covers. These, perhaps, were what one would grow up to. In the mean-time there was Ginger, and the gang.

The artistic separation in our family was a tripartite one. I was the reader and, for a brief time, during my poetry phase, the writer. My father was the artist, with considerable skill in catching a likeness with a pencil. My mother was the musician.

Like many other wartime households we had a tall upright piano, holding a proud position in the sitting-room. Ours was black, lacquery, and usually stood with the lid up, and some music on the folding stand; unlike many other households ours was one in which the piano was played.

My mother was a frequent, and a much sought-after, piano player. On the whole, at this period, the piano was seen as an adjunct to community singing rather than as the vehicle for a solitary recital, and what I remember best are crowded rooms with people leaning on the instrument's cornice, and my mother hammering out the tune of some popular hit.

Before the days of television, evening entertainment was more active, and I think more social, than it is nowadays. Few people would visit a neighbour to hear the news on the wireless, or to listen to a comedy show, but a gathering for a patriotic singsong was not uncommon.

Wind-up gramophones may have cut into this pursuit at a slightly later date, and with a slightly different age group, but these were chiefly associated with dancing, and thus with potential sexual partnerships between adolescents, or childless married couples. I don't think my parents, or for that matter their friends, would have regarded the physical closeness necessary for dancing as something that their young son should be made a party to.

Hence it was the direct, key-banging accompaniment of the piano to which people sang, and from which they picked up the tunes of the current hits, not the more abstract circling of the wax record, or the crackling airwave breaking of the wireless set, tuned to Hilversum or Luxembourg.

We did, in fact, possess a large Pye set in a Bakelite cabinet, with knurled knobs that allowed very careful alignment of wave-lengths, and this gave excellent reception, plugged, as it was, directly into the electricity supply at a point on the skirting-board.

Still, I never recall my mother listening to a popular song sung on the wireless. She evidently preferred to go out and buy the sheet music, and work out the tune for herself. It may be that this points to a period at which the song was still thought more interesting than the singer, or at any rate quite separable from any particular singer's interpretation of it.

Such a view was rapidly to change. Not only Marlene Dietrich with her definitive rendering of 'Lili Marlene', but Bing Crosby with his famous crooning, and soon Frank Sinatra with his fresh face and gesturing and, perhaps most of all, Vera Lynn, the Forces' sweetheart, were to alter the balance for ever.

My mother with her amateur concern to perfect the fingering herself, and then to voice her own interpretation of the words with her friends, was already an anachronism. The massive anonymity of the video single was looming on the horizon. Craft was passing into the hands of the professional.

We made our last trip up to Scotland by car for Easter in 1941. This was one of the comparatively rare occasions when we went as far as Dundee, to stay with my mother's older brother Jimmy, and his wife Isa.

The war at sea was now developing into a serious business, with transatlantic convoys threatened by the German submarine fleets. The British navy, albeit ensconced somewhat further north at Scapa Flow, seemed much more present in Dundee than anywhere else I had been.

There were long, sleek, grey battleships and destroyers with batteries of guns before and behind their funnels, and occasionally the broad, flat slope of an aircraft carrier's deck, with little aeroplanes rising from and falling towards it like flies.

There was also the boom, a line of barrels linked with a net of rope, stretching across the Firth of Tay to prevent the incursion of floating mines. Pictures of these, with their

sensitive antennae which would explode the device by some
kind of magnetic contact, had been published in magazines,
and I remember often looking down into the water from the
Tay Bridge in the hope of seeing one.

I never did, nor I think did anyone else in Dundee. This was
still the time when Britannia ruled the waves, at any rate
around the shores of our own island, if not in mid-ocean
beyond the Canaries, or to the north of Russia.

My Aunt Isa owned a hairdressing shop in Dundee, and I
was taken there to see my mother turned into a gigantic
insect, with her head invisible under the fearsome coping of
the drier. She came out looking much the same as before to
my crude male eye, but my three female cousins all highly
approved of her fashionable permanent wave.

These cousins were about six years older than I, and treated
me rather as a grown-up doll, to be prodded, admired and
examined. They all agreed, to my embarrassed horror, that I
had exceptionally long eyelashes, and that I would, when
older, be a great success with the girls.

There were two Scotties, too – Scottish terriers, to give
them their proper name – which I was allowed to take for
walks beside the river. I enjoyed the physical pull of their
necks on the rein, and even more the abstract responsibility,
albeit shared with some hovering adult, of making sure that
neither of them ran into the road, and in front of a car.

We no longer had any animals at home, not even a cat or a
bird, and I was probably a little starved for furry company. I
certainly invested a great deal of emotional enthusiasm in an
early teddy bear, and it became one of the only sources of
grievance I can readily recall against my mother.

One day it was judged that this silvery bear had either
grown too battered or too dirty to retain his place in a decent
household, and he was quietly removed, while I was asleep.

I was deeply shocked by this betrayal. I loved my bear, and
I couldn't understand why he had to go. His dirt and his
damage were of no significance to me. He was mine, my
closest friend, and the repository of many secrets unsuitable
for trusting to the ears of human adults.

Nevertheless, he was taken away, and I never saw him
again. Instead, the fur spaniel appeared, and I learned to zip

my pyjamas into his stomach, and grin and bear my loss. It wouldn't be the last.

Typing this book out, and realising that it will in time, after corrections, come to be retyped by a professional typist, I remember that my mother went to a secetarial college, and might easily, if she were alive still, be doing the job for me.

Three less than the year at the end of the year is always the way I used to calculate, and still do, my mother's age, since her birthday was in December. This would make her as I write these lines in her early eighties, and no doubt a spry, bony, gentle soul like her own mother.

Imagining her seated at a typewriter, and in an office, is something I find quite impossible. She certainly never owned an ancient Smith Corona or a lovingly preserved Remington in my time, unless it was very cleverly kept out of sight.

I suspect that she took the secretarial course, as many a girl might do today, without ever having much intention of practising the skills she would acquire there. Marriage, or at any rate courtship, no doubt intervened between the acquiring of the certificate of proficiency I still possess and the cold winds of need which might have sent her from door to bleak mahogany door in search of a job.

I don't suppose my father would have countenanced, or at least encouraged, the notion of a wife out at work. He would have been too keen to see himself in the role of sole provider, and my mother would surely have fallen in easily enough with this way of approaching matters.

Money was always attractive to my mother, but I'm sure she felt it should come from men, and not from her own efforts. Not that she was in any way lazy, the very reverse, but she saw the business of earning as a vulgarising affair for a woman.

Women were already appearing in offices, and my father certainly dealt with secretaries, though I never recall seeing one on my visits. I did hear some years ago of a young woman who had been at Colliery Engineering and remembered him as the nicest person she worked for there. His death came as a real grief to her. A more cynical mind than mine might be inclined to find material for some kind of extramarital connection in this episode. I don't seek any.

The marriage was a solid, and a happy, one. Despite the absence of physical affection in public, there were little signs which gave this away. The two sets of golf clubs, for example, supple and springy in their folding cloth bags, lay side by side and snuggled close in the attic.

I would sometimes be given a golf ball, torn in the side for some reason, and no longer of any use on the course. I would peel off the gutta-percha casing, like the outer skin of an orange, and finger the rippling ball of muscle packed in the interior. Layer upon layer it would unreel, fragmenting into little worms of broken elastic, until finally there at the centre I would come on the gooey final core, a white, sticky, disgusting precipitate, like dirty toothpaste.

Throughout the war, and afterwards, our houses were heated by coal fires. At Southbourne Road we had a fire in the sitting-room, although it was rarely lit, and one in the dining-room, which tended to double as a place to chatter or listen to the wireless after meals, and one in the kitchen.

There were also fires in the larger two of the three bedrooms upstairs, though not in the smallest room, which was mine. I never, even in the coldest winter weather, remember either of these upstairs fires being lit.

The way to keep warm in a bedroom was to climb into bed and snuggle down under the blankets with a hot-water bottle. We had some old stone ones, with stubby snouts and humped, rounded earthenware backs. These were known as pigs, no doubt commemorating some lost agricultural era when a Scotsman would retire to his straw in the company of a hot young sow.

We also, of course, possessed the more cuddlesome rubber variety, which would sometimes leak, or even burst, with a concomitant flooding of the sheets akin to bed-wetting.

Coal for the downstairs fires would be delivered at regular intervals in a heaped lorry that stood at the front gate while soot-blackened men carried sacks up the drive on their backs and then tipped them out with a scrambling crunch into the cellar. This cellar, though part of the house, was a paltry affair compared with the great underground cavern in the Crescent. It amounted to no more than a windowless closet.

My mother, like most women of the time, harboured a perennial suspicion that the coalmen would attempt to cheat her by some stratagem such as supplying a nineteen- rather than a twenty-bag ton. So she always insisted that I help her by doing a count of the bags as we heard them shouldered off and showered down on the pile.

She did her own count, too, and this was felt to provide a double check. I don't ever recall the coalmen giving us short measure. They were usually a dour, frozen couple, no doubt with a long round to complete before their teatime.

Only at Christmas did they appear in a more smiling light, when they came to the back door after the delivery, and waited expectantly for the traditional annual gratuity. No one would ever have dared to stint on this offering. It would have been remembered, and paid for.

Such, at any rate, was the general assumption. The other tradesmen thought to require a Christmas sweetening were the milkman, who arrived so early that we never saw him, and the bin-men, whose power to impose sanctions, embedded in the opportunity to abandon us in the contagious effluvia of uncollected rubbish, always appeared exceptionally strong. They were the most generously remunerated at this season by my mother.

The bin-men were also known as the dustmen, and I realise that this is because the bulk of our garbage in those days comprised the ash and embers from our coal fires. So much came back to heating, and the necessity for it, that our minds were well attuned to the dangers of naked flame.

I was well tutored in how important it was to put guards round the grate, to snatch up any cinder that fell on the carpet, and to make sure that the gas for the cooker was properly turned off.

When winter approached, these precautions, and the threat they envisaged, assumed a more public resonance as we waited for a renewal of the German air raids. The fear of a conflagration was probably a more clearly framed one than the psychological horror of a gas attack. Certainly, as much damage was done by the narrow finned cylinders of the German incendiary bombs as by the fatter, more obscenely suggestive devices which delivered high explosives.

One night my father went out to help some people across the road put out an incendiary bomb that had fallen on their house. I don't know what he did, or with what success, but there was later an overheard remark that he should have got a medal.

In my boyhood dreams of dramatic achievement, this made my father a hero. I cherished the remark.

Playing cards were often considered in Scottish households as the picture book of the devil. I don't think this view was held in my own family, because we did in fact own, and sometimes use, several decks of cards.

Bridge was not much played, but whist was, and I recall serious, frowning faces around the frayed baize of a cross-legged, folding card-table. This was also used for games of draughts, or dominoes, and later for more recent amusements such as the Frenchified game, L'Attaque, which involved rather irritatingly collapsible cardboard warriors on little metal supports, and some grandiose military plan of campaign I now forget.

Monopoly was just coming in, and indeed may well have begun to assume the proportions of a craze. I was allowed to watch my parents playing this fascinatingly incomprehensible game with some friends, late one Saturday night. The game was taking place in their house, and I had been loaned a miniature mouth-organ to keep me amused.

For some reason it seems to have found its way into my trouser pocket, and was there ignominiously discovered, fortunately before we left for home. My father was much upset by this evidence of larceny, and my plea of boredom and forgetfulness was not taken very seriously.

At home, there were games of rummy, and snap, and hands of a Walt Disney game called Dumbo, with rather gaudy cards of the flying baby elephant and his friends to be collected in suits.

One of the most mysterious uses of cards, though, and one

which may well account for their association with the black arts of magic, was their employment to tell fortunes.

Astrology, the favoured superstition of the present day, was less popular in the 1940s when, after all, you were more likely to see a Dornier bomber than a pot of gold in the stars. Reading tea-leaves, when the draining of a cup would create a complex pattern arranged around the sides of the china, was much more commonplace.

Weddings and inheritances were frequently foreshadowed in the after-leavings of a good brew of Typhoo. But it was the playing cards, and their arcane meanings, to which most careful attention was paid.

I still possess a family set of fortune cards, all cased in a thin gold card-case, and each marked with a written interpretation of the suit and value it bears. The backs of the cards are decorated with seven-branched candlesticks, and I never look at them now without a shudder.

One night in early October of 1941 my father had his fortune read by the simple, familiar method of turning up a card from a cut deck. He turned up the ace of spades.

There were always ways, then as now, of avoiding the brutal implications of a death card, and I have no doubt those present were well able to make out some symbolic change rather than some ultimate fate in this desolating card.

At any rate, it was never mentioned until later. Later, it was remembered, and mentioned with fear, and with awe.

10

The sirens began to call again in September, and we were ready for them. Everyone, I think, expected that this might be another winter of heavy raids. Perhaps because of our previous good fortune in enjoying the protection of the hall corner my father had so far not invested in an Anderson shelter.

What he had done was to order the supposedly more up-to-date Morrison shelter, named after the Herbert Morrison who succeeded Sir John Anderson as Home Secretary, and in due course one of these did arrive. It was a massive, bolted, iron construction in the form of a large table, which you put inside your house, and which was guaranteed to support the weight of some vast number of crumbled tons of masonry.

Ours replaced the dining-room table, and stood with a decorative rug across its forbidding back until it was finally dismantled in 1945. It was fun to play under, unless you sat up sharply and banged your head on cold iron.

At this date, however, we were still relying on the hall, albeit with one little novelty to keep war at a distance. The magic sound of the sirens, and the artillery of aerial battle, could now be excluded from consciousness, at least to some extent, by the insertion of small, golden rubbery plugs into one's ears. They were shaped like tiny, pliable chessmen.

My father, like Ulysses who tied his men to the mast and bound their eyes to prevent enchantment, insisted that my mother and I wear these itchy stoppers. But he disdained their use himself, and indeed spent little time at home. On Home Guard duty he preferred to be out in the streets, a prey to whatever seductive influence the sirens might offer.

One night, on 20 October 1941, nine days after his thirty-seventh birthday, he had heard the air-raid warning, seen that my mother and I were safely tucked into the usual hall corner, and had then put on his uniform and gone round to the office.

I have an impression that he was on fire-fighting duty, though it may seem strange that he should have had to put on his uniform for this. I think actually that he liked wearing the uniform. It made him feel part of the war.

I can understand this feeling. My father had every right to his uniform, and there was a war on, and I don't grudge him his chance to dress for what was going to happen. But I do envy him.

At any rate, he went out, not too late in the evening, and walked towards the office. I don't know whether he ever got there, or whether he arrived and left later. But he never came back.

Sometimes I think that I heard the shell, sometimes I even think that my mother says I mentioned hearing it. It may be so, I don't know any more. The next things I remember are all from the following chapter, the long, still unfinished chapter of everything that has happened since my father died.

I suppose someone must have come to the door. I don't remember. I do remember my mother being asked to come across the road to the house of some friends, and I know that I went over with her.

These friends had a son who later lent me some Edwardian children's books, mostly by Henty, with patriotic themes and illustrations showing the grander military exploits in English history. Their house was a middle-sized stone one with a well-cultivated garden leading up to the front door.

It probably seemed a long walk for my mother that night. I expect she already guessed why she was going. My memory is of a number of men in the narrow hall, and of someone asking me to wait in a front room. Probably someone came in and talked to me. I don't remember.

What I do remember is hearing something I'd never heard before — the sound of my mother crying, somewhere in the distance. Then, a little later, someone came in and said that I had to be a brave boy from now on and look after my mother, because my father was dead.

I don't recall it as being a shock. It was too soon, and I was perhaps too young, to feel any sense of grief. I went through to the other room and there was my mother, and she was crying, and she was alive, and I sat down beside her, and she put her arms round me, and I suppose I tried to say whatever a boy of nine years who has just lost his father tries to say to his mother, who has just lost the man she loves.

I didn't cry. I thought it was important not to cry. Boys didn't cry. My father had died, and he was a hero, but that wasn't something to cry about.

This all happened over forty-five years ago as I type these lines, and things have changed. I haven't struck a single letter without seeing the keys blinded by tears.

I learned later what had happened. I think I picked it up from overhearing what people were saying, in hushed voices, in the corridor. In particular I remember the voice of Mr Speakman, a rather stout, florid man whom I associate with check suits and a slightly bookmakerish manner, who was dressed rather incongruously this evening in wellington boots.

Speakman was the traveller for Colliery Engineering. He is always present in my mind with an impressive car, and I believe that his salary lay in an undefined, but attractive, region somewhere between that of my father and Laurie himself.

Neither Speakman, as I always heard him called, nor any of the other men present was in uniform. I heard someone say, or later, I thought I did, that the head had been severed. I think this came up over the question of my mother going to identify the body. Nobody wanted her to have to do this, and I don't know whether she did or not.

What had happened, seemingly, is that an anti-aircraft shell had failed to explode in the sky. It had gone up and then come down in Clarkehouse Road where my father was walking. It had either fallen very near, or actually struck him. There are several versions. Across the road another man, a complete stranger, was also killed.

The following day there was a report on the two deaths on the front page of the evening paper, the *Sheffield Star*. No other people had been killed that night. In fact, although there had been an air-raid warning, no bombs had been dropped.

Years later my headmaster, Dr Barton, wrote to me with what he thought was sympathy, describing my father's death as a distressing accident. I was annoyed by this. I didn't regard my father's death as an accident. I felt that he'd been killed in the front line, fighting Fascism. I still feel this.

Fortunately, my view was shared by the British Government, who saw to it that my mother was paid a soldier's pension. This struck me as a mark of honour, as well as a financial convenience, and I was always proud, as well as amused, when in due course I drew this for myself.

It may be that, ever prudent, my father had foreseen the economic advantages of being killed with khaki on one's back, and that this was one of his motives in making sure that he never went out during an air raid without this useful insurance. I like to think so.

Romantic attachment to the world of military splendour may not necessarily be inconsistent with a stoutly practical sense of the value of money.

Sometimes I go back to Sheffield now and walk along Clarkehouse Road to the place where I think my father must have fallen. I don't know exactly where it was, but I believe it to have been within the half-circle made by the wall leading to the classical gates of the Botanical Gardens.

It strikes me as a noble place to have been killed. Sometimes I try to work out the exact spot where my father died. I've even stopped, when I thought no one was watching, and touched the pavement. I have a dream that there might be a tiny fleck of his blood still there, dyed for ever into the stone.

But I never found one.

The Iron Lung

Along that ward men died each winter night.
     One in an iron lung
Used to cry out before that salving tin
Strapped round his breathing stifled him. One hung
     In a strange brace
That moved his dead leg gently. And no light
    Out of that blaze where Hitler in
His burning concrete died lit the cramped face

Of a boy paralysed. I in that war
     Lay with cold steel on wrists
Recording how my heart beat, saved and one
With the men dying. Dark amidst the mists
     Across the seas
Each night in France those armies gripped and tore
    Each other's guts out, and no sun
Arched in at dawn through stiff windows to ease

Men left in pain. Sisters on morning rounds
     Brought laundered sheets and screens
Where they were needed. And when doctors came
In clean coats with their talk and their machines,
     Behind their eyes
Moving to help, what was there? To the sounds
    Of distant gunfire, in our name,
So many men walked into death. What lies

And festers is the wastage. Here the beast
     Still breathes its burning stone
And claws the entrails. And those hours of cold
When I lay waking, hearing men alone
     Fight into death
Swim back and grip. And I feel rise like yeast
    A sense of the whole world grown old
With no-one winning. And I fight for breath.

11

I don't know who made the arrangements for the funeral, but they were soon in hand. What I chiefly remember is that this was the first and only occasion on which any of my Scottish relations came down to England.

Indeed, this was perhaps the central symbol of how my father's death was to reverse many of the traditional structures of my life.

The circumstances under which my relations were bedded and boarded remain obscure. I'm not even quite sure how many came. I certainly have an image of Marie, my cousin, who must then have been a young woman in her mid-twenties. Rather unfairly — since she is now most affable and generous to me — I remember her pulling my hair and pinching me in my mother's bedroom.

Perhaps she felt that I needed to be snapped out of my gloom, or distracted from the more hideous elements in the family mulling-over of the paraphernalia of death in the sitting-room down below. My Cousin Margaret, her sister, also there, and younger, I recall acting as a moderating influence. Perhaps the two girls were acting in concert, on the principle of matching the stick with the carrot.

Later Margaret was to become a particularly dab hand with a carrot. She was educated in the culinary arts at what my aunts used to call the Dough School, or Domestic Science College, in Glasgow, and to judge from Margaret, they knew their business.

The figure I remember most prominently from the funeral, though, is my Uncle David, the eldest of my mother's two surviving brothers. Uncle David, though a furniture dealer like his brother Jimmy, and a man with a family reputation for sharp practice, had a most saintly and distinguished appearance, as if he were a bishop at a christening.

This manner, coated with a filament of discreet melancholy, was rather appropriate for a funeral, and I find that in retrospect I am almost starring my Uncle David as the presiding clergyman at the service. He wasn't, of course, and he can't have been, and, as I wasn't allowed for some compassionate, though I now think misconceived, reason to attend the burial, I wouldn't even know if he had been.

The image of 'oor Davey', as he always emerges in my memory of family reference, is that of a large man with folded hands appraising the chairs from a comfortable vantage point in a corner. This noted practice, and his probably disinterested offer to help my mother in any valuation she might need to make for probate of my father's will, was later held against him by my Aunt Margaret, a woman not easy on sactimoniousness.

Aunt Margaret — rather confusingly not the mother of Cousin Margaret — was inclined to think that Uncle David would be quick to make some profitable offer for any superfluous items that my mother might want to dispose of. In fact, there were no such items, and so far as I know Uncle David's offer was never taken up.

Mutual suspicion was a common feature of the Mann family, as I observed them from my childhood position of being seen but not heard. However, I feel bound to record in his favour that my Uncle David was the most generous of several affluent and beneficent uncles.

I never visited, or met, him without coming away with a crackling paper gratuity, either the rusty orange of a ten-shilling note or the watery green of a whole pound. On one momentous occasion, later objected to by my mother for its potential corrupting power, I found the tight white wad of a five-pound note folded into my surreptitious hand.

Allowing for inflation, this would have to be the present-day equivalent of something between fifty and a hundred pounds. No wonder my mother felt that I might have my head swollen by such terrible wealth.

There was always an art in accepting money from adults. You would hang about, nonchalantly but politely, to the rear of a group leaving a room, and thus allow the potential donor both the time and the opportunity to reach into his pocket or wallet – it was always a man, incidentally – and extract whatever gratuity had been chosen as most suitable.

Then you would approach with eyes modestly cast down and, murmuring a pleasant farewell, make as if to pass by without shaking hands while, at the same time, allowing one ready fist to trail helpfully alongside trouser crease or open pocket.

The adult would then feel both delighted by your absence of any gross air of expectancy, and at the same time free to slide the decided sum easily into either your palm or your trouser pocket. Both methods were, in fact, used.

My Uncle Hugh was the only man I knew who scorned these mutually agreed subterfuges, and who seemed to delight in the flagrant waiving of conventions, reaching over, and sometimes even shouting out, 'Here, George, here's something for you', as he pressed magnificent largesse upon me.

I think I had more money from my Uncle Hugh than from any other of my adult benefactors. He was a man, I believe, who knew the value of money, and who loved the extravagance of watching it move through its paces, creating luxury and delight.

I always saw him as a Victorian capitalist, a self-made millionaire who owned a house he had built himself next door to Johnny Walker, the whisky king, and who ran his own horses in the Derby, and who showed me once in the back of his chauffeur-driven Humber a small table that unfolded and became a cocktail cabinet.

I think he must have been down for the funeral, but I have no memory of his massive bulk, or his wavy hair, or his tiger's smile that runs out still like a flash of claws in his grandchildren, or his huge, raw, Aberdeen granite voice, as warm and as powerful as a brazier on a building site.

It was Aunt Marian who was my mother's eldest sister, and an iodine-fine woman, with a humorous dryness that seems now a perfect foil for her flamboyant husband. I see her always in the background, a slight prune of a lady in later years, too old for me to feel at ease with.

But I know how close they were. After her death, my Uncle Hugh went every day to the cemetery, to take fresh

flowers to her grave. That sets an example, and one that snags
at my mind over many neglectful years.

My mother and I must have started to take flowers to my
father's grave fairly soon. I have memories of the long walk
up the hill to Crosspool, and then to Crookes, where the
public cemetery lies on its hill, overlooking, now, a valley
with much new building.

There was always the valley, but in earlier days it was full of
trees. I would go through the lines of memorials hunched up
in my raglan overcoat, or neat and sweating in my school
blazer, armed with roses or daffodils to remember my father
at all seasons, rain or fine, my mother beside me – at first in
her dark mourning clothes, and later in brighter colours, but
always tall, and beautiful, and a little quieter than usual.

There were never tears, nor was there ever any talk of my
father. We would discuss the weather, or the best way to
arrange the flowers, and then I would help throw away any
earlier, withered ones, carrying them in my arms to a tin
waste-basket, while my mother waited alone at the grave.

What she said, or thought, or did, in those few moments
alone I don't know. But there were still no tears when we
turned to come away, into the wind or the sun, returning
through the world of the dead to our shaken, and yet not
shattered, world of home and school, and the network of the
family, and living on.

The Chalmers had a house at Crosspool, and we often
stopped there on our way back for a cup of tea, and so that I
could play with Eveline. I think my mother liked to hear Mr
Chalmers talk of my father, which he always did in terms of
an awed respect.

Eveline and I would sometimes be sent out for some chips,
and it may be that more serious, or more tearful, talk took
place on these private occasions. But I suspect not. My
mother was a proud woman, and she wanted to keep my
father to herself.

It was all right, indeed rather pleasant, to hear people praise
him casually in public, but his private virtues, whatever these
were, should remain her own secret, and her own privilege.

12

After the funeral the confusing family went home. Some will have travelled by train; a few, I suppose, in their own luxurious cars. Aunt Margaret, I suspect, stayed on for a while.

She was always the closest of my mother's relations. Widowed, as she had been early in her marriage, she would presumably have seemed a natural companion for my mother at such a time. Neither her son, my Cousin Jimmy, nor her daughter, my Cousin May, features in my recollections of this period, but they were ten or more years older than I, and may have been away at school, or left in Scotland with friends.

Aunt Margaret is often alone in my mind. She was a formidable, ferocious woman in many ways, with an active golfer's physique, and a quick, impetuous temper.

She had a powerful organising mind and, later in the war, when she worked for the Food Office, came to rule over the whole empire of rationing in Hamilton, and would travel in an official car to discuss and dispense quotas with deferential grocers. If ever there was to be a little bit extra available after the just apportionment of the customer's dues, then this would find its way, very often, to my aunt's visiting basket in the shape of a half-pound of butter, or a box of Highland cream toffees.

This made her a delightful companion for a small boy who was starved of sweets, and who came to see her occasional surfeit of these commodities as a splendid cornucopia.

I think my aunt was in many ways a disappointed and, some might say, even a bitter woman. She had a sharp tongue, and a fearless disposition. Unlike many women of her time, she was never afraid to mix it in a row with a man.

Later, when her daughter married an English soldier, and I was present as a guest at the wedding in my first three-piece suit, I wrote a comic account of the ceremony which I was ill-advised to show to my aunt for her, as I hoped, approval. I was astonished to be treated to a sharp sermon on the vice of ingratitude.

Although she knew of, and respected, and indeed assisted, my ambitions to be a writer, my aunt was incapable of grasping that I was simply flexing my muscles, trying my wings as a sort of Dickensian commentator. What I wrote bore no more relation to the reality of the wedding than a prentice bodice-ripper to the business of sex.

Whereas I, who had enjoyed the wedding, and felt proud to have been invited, and was indeed grateful for the good food I had eaten, had no idea that she could fail to see the difference between a boring documentary report of an event and the necessary adornments of a piece of literature.

It has taken me many years to see that my aunt was right, and I was wrong.

The financial pressures of my father's death must have borne heavily on my mother. I don't really know, and suppose I never will, how she managed to make up for the £750 a year of which she had been deprived.

Our sources of income are clear. We had my father's pension, from the government. He had none from his office, at least officially, though I believe some means to help a little may have been found.

These sources would hardly have made up for a salary. My own good fortune in winning a scholarship meant that the fees for school were paid for, but not, I think, all the clothes, including the sports things, that a growing boy would need.

Nevertheless, we managed to live, and in what I still remember as style. Perhaps the main concession to a genteel financial embarrassment was our taking in of a lodger, a prim, schoolmistressish lady called Miss Green.

Miss Green — who must have possessed a Christian name, but I never heard it — was more like a schoolmistress than any schoolmistress I have ever known. In fact, she was the headmistress of a primary school, and a very tidy, self-reliant individual who made an excellent and not very obtrusive addition to the household.

She rented two rooms: the dining-room with the table

shelter downstairs, and the front or visitor's bedroom upstairs, with its morosely dark suite of mahogany furniture. I would sometimes peek in and marvel at the summary detritus of an alien female's clothing, though it was rarely anything more exotic than a pair of dreary slippers or a plaid wool dressing-gown.

Miss Green was also, of course, allowed to wash in the bathroom and, more controversially and potentially acrimoniously, cook in the kitchen. There were days of complaints, but on the whole the arrangement seems to have worked out quite well, since Miss Green remained, as I remember, until well after the war.

It must have been hard, though, for my mother to accept the notion of another woman living as a paying guest in her own house. As a minor capitalist, with her own row of houses in Scotland, she would have accepted the idea of renting out property, but hardly part of the house you lived in yourself.

The houses in May Street can hardly have yielded much income. By the time they passed into my own and my cousins' hands, much later on, they were dilapidated to the point of being condemned, and a holding company had had to be formed to prevent we owners from becoming liable for heavy repair bills.

In fact, a thin trickle of cheques did leak south, but these were the profits of disposal, by gradual sale to sitting tenants, and they never bought me more than a few extra train journeys. I doubt if ever they did more for my mother.

It was saving, and home cooking, and not going out, and a genius for keeping accounts and finding bargains, that made our life in England comfortable, and even, fairly frequently, still enabled us to go back to Scotland.

Now that we no longer owned the Standard 9 – since neither my mother nor I could drive it, the car had been sold – we were compelled to make our trips up to Scotland by train.

Trains in the early 1940s, as I remember them, were invariably crowded. Most of them were of the corridor and compartment sort, with a comfortable four seats to a side, if the moquette arms were folded up into the wall. There was a central outside window that ran down by lifting a thong like a razor strop from its position over a miniature brass capstan.

Usually, there were more than eight seated people in a compartment, and sometimes, on shorter journeys, even a few standing as well. Many of these were in uniform: soldiers with kitbags returning from leave, ATS girls on their way to new postings, or sailors with rectangular white collars like Edwardian children, staring silently ahead as they contemplated months at sea on a troop-ship or an MTB.

The withdrawal from Dunkirk seemed to have filled England with service people, many of them apparently with little to do except be shunted from one grim transit camp to another, always borne down under an impossible weight of military luggage.

No doubt many of the army rearrangements were designed to re-equip depleted units abroad, but the total number of figures in England in khaki seemed always to remain about the same, and most of them evidently had to travel on the same trains and at the same times as we did.

The one category of military figures rarely seen at a station was an airman, and this helped, I suppose, to form my distorted view that the war was being won for us almost entirely in the air. The glamour of the RAF was a powerful thing in the 1940s, and the famous phrase of Churchill's about the many never before having owed so much to so few had taken a deep root.

At the economic level, the many had not been accustomed to owing much in England to the few – rather the reverse, in fact. An echo of the class system which supported the good fortune of the oppressive few survived in the division of the trains into first, second and third classes, though I saw nothing of first and second. We always travelled third.

I know now that officers always travelled first, and this accounts for the fact that I saw so few of them in my time on the trains north. It made the army seem much more dramatic, and overburdened with luggage, and level in rank, than it really was.

As a consequence of the overcrowding, there had to be a good deal of squashing up. It was not uncommon for a small boy like myself to feel like the thin slice of Spam in a particularly thick-cut sandwich where the two slices of bread were represented by enormous corporals.

I resented the anonymous juxtaposition of male flesh, but there was little I could do about it. At a later date, with the approach of puberty, I was to grow much happier at the prospect of travelling on crowded trains, and would angle for a seat alongside a seductive WAAF, or a plump-thighed civilian secretary in a short skirt.

My earliest experiences of sexual pleasure in the presence of women came, I suppose, from such delightful, though of course publicly ignored, alignments. I became a connoisseur of pressure of young flesh through skirt and trouser leg, and would focus my attention, sometimes for hours, on the question of whether the adjacent lady was appreciating the experience as much as I was.

I'm sure she usually wasn't. A small and grubby boy in a blazer with a book would hardly have appealed as much as a talkative, or even a dormant, artillery sergeant, or a muscular private from the Catering Corps.

Nevertheless, despite my own care to make no movement – I was far too frightened for that – I occasionally had the sense that some no doubt lecherous or deprived girl was pressing closer. On the few occasions when I stole a covert look sideways to check on this, the woman in question would invariably, alas, turn out to be frumpish, dozing, or old.

Once or twice a pretty girl standing nearby would seem to lean the back of a silk-stockinged knee against my thigh, but this could be attributed to mere tiredness at having to support her own weight, and the interpretation of a tribute to my masculinity or sexual appeal was thus ruled out.

Reflecting on my own pubescent behaviour on the trains, it occurs to me that my mother, an attractive woman in her later thirties, may very well have been considerably bothered by the attentions of men.

What I would allow to happen, and indeed mildly encourage, out of a burgeoning adolescent lust may have been more actively and skilfully cultivated by older and bolder seducers.

I saw no signs of anything that might have been construed

as an attempt to pick my mother up, but then we are dealing here with an area of preliminary, or even alternative, persecution, easy to disguise and awkward to combat.

Indeed, remembering the long shuttling through night-black tunnels with no lights on in the compartments, I can see that there would have been ample opportunity for what might be called a grope in the dark.

My mother was a figure of much dignity, however, and I suspect that few ordinary soldiers, unless extremely drunk, would have seen her as the potential target for such a blatant approach. Perhaps it would have been different in a first-class carriage.

In general, between consenting adults, the 1940s was a period of much more overt and physical sexual contact than the 1980s has come to be. This is often forgotten. It may be that far more is done in private nowadays than during the war, and between far more couples, but our public tolerance of even kissing, not to mention heavy petting, has been drastically reduced.

Perhaps the shortness of meetings, combined with the lack of places to go, made young lovers more ready to express their feelings in the presence of others. I certainly remember seeing quite serious bouts of what one might call foreplay taking place on platforms, in the corridors of trains, and in the corner seats of carriages, and no one seemed to feel that this was the sort of thing a young boy should be shielded from.

A film such as *Brief Encounter* sums up the mood of the time. There was a frailty in human connection which could so easily be severed by the snapped thread of a new posting or, worse, the bloody segmentation of a falling doodlebug, or a V2. You had to love where you could.

My mother was a living example of the love that had already suffered its final severance, and yet had to survive, somehow, and soldier on. In this, she was a typical figure.

The sense of my mother's sexuality is a troubled one. Until quite an advanced age, I don't think that I'd seen her without her clothes on, and I never ever saw her undressed except in the bath.

Once or twice, as I grew older, she would invite me to wash her back, and I remember vividly the ogival ridge of her spine, rising to a long hoop of articulated stones, like the close beads of an amber necklace, as she leaned forward and exposed a wide swath of stretched skin, like the surface of a kite, or a shield, for me to soap.

I have always felt a rush of tenderness when I see the back of a woman's neck, and her stooping shoulders, and this must date, I suppose, from these early experiences of helping my mother to clean those parts of her body most difficult to reach.

The front of my mother's body remained a sheltered mystery. I was never invited to wash in front, or even to look there. From the one or two quick glances I took when her hands were otherwise engaged than in covering herself – an instinctive urge towards modesty, and one universal in her age and class – I remember the surprising, unpleasing folds of her breasts, loops of loose skin, as they seemed to me, and with little relevance either to the firm flatness of my own chest or the swollen mammary splendours of pin-up girls such as Evelyn Keyes or Betty Grable, which I had seen hinted at under bursting sweaters in the inner pages of tabloid news-papers.

This helps to remind me that my mother was a beauty of the 1920s, a 'flapper', I suppose, who had acquired her bosom at a period when the straight-up-and-down look was the one most prized.

Nakedness, of course, was not, as it is not with the adult Japanese, the most immediate trigger of sexual response to a boy of my age. I was bred on the excitements of a flashing calf with a stocking seam, or the sway of a tweed-skirted bottom above clicking stiletto heels.

The exaggerations of these allurements among the very young, as glimpsed in the street, or as pictured in magazines, did little to prepare me for any prurient stimulus in my mother's clothing. She often wore silk stockings, but also sometimes lisle ones. They were supported, I assume, by a suspender belt, but I never saw one of these, either on or off.

Knickers there but, but these, though a theoretically appealing peach colour, and a heavy satin material, were longer than my utilitarian football shorts, which were also known as knickers, and also elasticated at the waist. The one feature of my mother's rather secretive bloomers which strikes me in retrospect as having had any libidinous content was the elastic leg-fringes, which made them grip just above the knee and thus conceal any bare area above the stocking top.

Amazing that what should have been designed so practically to hide, and to keep warm, should be what remains as most immediately titillating. But then these were years when the mystery was infinitely more erotic than the revelation.

As for my mother's shoes, to conclude my survey of her amatory wardrobe, these were invariably discreet, elegant and enclosed, allowing no peep of painted toe, or curl of dimpled heel. And they were comparatively low. No self-respecting siren, such as Rita Hayworth, or Jane of the *Daily Mirror*, would have been seen dead in them. Or alive either, for that matter.

As in everything else, my mother comes back as a model of good taste. I wonder sometimes how I could have borne it if she had been fortunate enough to meet some lover sufficiently tender and persistent to court her with a decorum equal to her own.

Luckily for me, this was never put to the test. She never did.

13

Normally, we would arrive in Scotland at the station in Glasgow, travel on by bus to Hamilton, and then walk the remainder of the way to my grandmother's house down Douglas Street.

Nowadays a pair of semi-detached monstrosities lies on the site of Kinburn Lodge, and the broad spread of waste ground falling away to the side of it — where I used to watch men illegally playing pontoon for money, and snatching up their cards to run when word reached them that 'the poliss' were coming — has been levelled, and tarmacked, and turned into a car park.

Hamilton is little more than a fast one-way system for traffic *en route* to the M40, hurtling at seventy miles per hour past the remains of what was once the great house of the Duke of Hamilton, obliviously breaking right through the mere unmarked space in air where I climbed down to the fascinating river from Bothwell Bridge.

One of the few things which has not changed is the ground used by the Hamilton Academicals Football Club — always known as the Accies.

In my day, it was possible to climb up the dusty stairs to our attic, and stand on a chest for a view through the skylight of one-half of the pitch. Hence, you had a good understanding of exactly fifty per cent of the game. As they say, half a loaf is better than no bread, and a Scotsman always enjoys an entertainment he hasn't had to pay for, however inconvenient it may have been to arrange.

When my father was alive, my Cousin Jimmy would have come out in his kilt and drawn back the wrought-iron gates to let our car in. I can still hear the scrunch of them on the gravel.

Now we simply walked through. The gates were permanently folded back. The house itself was a squarish, plain stone building, with a basement, a *piano nobile*, a bedroom floor and an attic. It was double-fronted, with a flight of steps flanked by a solid balustrade leading up to an imposing door.

Round the back there were various, in my time always dilapidated, outbuildings, including a cobwebby wash-house, with a rusted iron wringer. I only knew my Aunt Margaret do the washing indoors, wringing on a movable mangle attached to the edge of the Belfast sink, and some-times thrashing water out of the drenched clothes in a tin bath with a posher – a sort of copper colander on the end of a pole.

Kinburn Lodge had fallen on hard times. After my grand-father's failure, a number of economies were introduced, including the letting of the ground floor and basement to another family. In my time, this was never spoken of, nor do I recall seeing this family.

We would pass through the front door and climb the curving stairway to the first floor as if this were the most natural thing in the world, and the hall and large rooms on either side of it non-existent.

I found the stairway gloomy and overbearing. All the way up there were large oils in complex gilded frames depicting stags or dogs in Highland landscapes. My grandfather had been a picture dealer, and I have every reason to suppose that these despised canvases – despised by the adults as well as feared by me – were works likely nowadays to command substantial sums in the auction rooms. But not in those days. The 1940s witnessed the nadir of Victoriana.

At the top of the stairs there was a broad, open hall, covered with linoleum and red carpeting. From this, rooms led off on all sides. To the far left there was what used to be the bedroom shared by my mother and me, with the bathroom and lavatory next door. Then there was my grandmother's room, my Aunt Margaret's room, the sitting-room, a flight of further stairs to the attic, and finally a sort of dining-room or parlour with a kitchen leading off behind it, half-concealed by a curtain.

The scale of Kinburn Lodge, after the simplicity of life in all the houses I knew in England, always impressed me. The style of life there, however, did not. There was no vestige of luxury, of the kind enjoyed by my Uncle Hugh, for example, at The Cairns.

Rather the opposite. Everything seemed old, and worn. The garden was untended, and full of thick black slugs, which you would come upon unexpectedly in long grass. They effectively prevented me from playing there.

Whenever it rained — which was often — everyone would run round with buckets and jugs to catch the water dripping — sometimes even flooding — down the walls. I doubt if there had been any money to spend on the roof for the last ten years.

My grandmother was an ancient, deaf presence, in a series of ragged-seeming, though I suspect fastidiously preserved, black dresses. I found her frightening, perhaps considering her like the witch in *Snow White*, and disliked the curious decrepit odour that always seemed to cling to her.

Children are notoriously antagonistic to dark colours, and decay, and often to great age, too, but I blame myself for conforming so simply to the banal norm.

There would have been much I could have learned from my grandmother. She might have opened up the whole of Victorian Scotland, like a princess putting a key to a magic drawer. She might even have told me who painted those awesome, wonderful pictures on the stairs. Now I shall never know.

Exactly when my grandmother died I don't now remember. When I knew her she was always dying, not in the way the rest of us are, by slow and imperceptible stages, but with a steady, progressive, stately decline.

One year there must have been some sudden acceleration in this, and I recall a whole visit in the course of which I never saw her. No doubt our trip had been aimed to coincide with, and perhaps solace if it could, the terminal phase of her last illness.

I have no idea what this illness was, or indeed if it was any kind of illness at all other than the weakness of advanced old age. My grandmother comes back to me as well over eighty, and her movements, at any rate in my presence, appeared stricken by a decrepitude of slowness.

On the other hand, hindsight, accompanied by the limited and scary information of adulthood, has inclined me to recall that sinister smell, and to create the spectre of her having suffered from cancer. This would not, of course, be surprising. Many old people do, and my grandmother, to add one crumb of little learning to another, was terribly thin.

These much advertised symptoms were not the most noticeable ones of the only woman I did watch failing from cancer at close quarters, but there are many varieties of this haunting disease, and the absorbed horrors of a worried folk mythology remain.

I remember the door of my grandmother's bedroom permanently closed, except when someone — never me — would pass through with a tray of food, or a bottle of medicine. Sometimes there would be a visit from the doctor, with his chunky miniature Gladstone bag, and his air of easy *bonhomie* which fooled nobody.

So my grandmother died, and this was the end of another era. My Aunt Margaret, who had lived in the house with her, and endured, no doubt, many years of worry and irritation, became the mistress of Kinburn Lodge.

It was not, as I have suggested, a particularly grandiose, or even enviable, position. Rather the opposite. Indeed, I imagine my aunt would readily have disposed of the leaking mansion to the first-comer, if she had been able in wartime to find anyone likely to buy it.

The 1940s was the epoch when nineteenth-century artefacts were at their lowest ebb, and a rotting, dank, partly rented-out and unheatable stucco house from the 1880s was hardly likely to fetch a price high enough to meet the cost of acquiring a tenement flat.

So my aunt, with her two growing children, and her dreams, no doubt, of earlier Edwardian splendours, had to linger on in the ruins of glory as she may have conceived them, scratching a pathetic living on a morass of mould and a chamber of echoes.

After the war, when both her children were married, she would move to a much smaller house in the Bothwell Road, and I would see her holding court over a remembered row of D. K. Broster novels, and a brass-plated scuttle for coal with a sloping roof and a relief of Highland cattle.

However, the enormous pictures from the stairway,

whoever they were by, were never moved. It may be that they were snapped up for some bargain price by my enterprising Uncle David. It may be, more probably, that they were knocked down at auction for a few shillings, and lay for long years rotting away in some dusty attic.

I like to think of them re-emerging, a little the worse for wear, but still retouchable, and making someone's fortune in the mid-1970s. Alas, it will not have been my Aunt Margaret's. By then she was out of her mind, and in an old people's home.

My experience of funerals has been a wide one. As a child, however, it was the *après-ski* period of the baked meats and the spiteful threnodies rather than the downhill skimming to the brink of the furnace or the fresh-cut grave that I was familiar with.

It doesn't seem to have been the thing in our family for small boys to attend the church ceremonies featuring the last rites. On the other hand, there was no bar, provided one kept one's mouth shut, on overhearing the lengthy harangues or whispered gossip which would always accompany the cheerful eating up of mutton pies and jelly pieces after the corpse had been satisfactorily disposed of.

My grandmother's funeral was one I missed. Perhaps we had to return to England for the beginning of a new school term. Perhaps my mother simply didn't feel up to another raking-over of old scores or a ransacking of older cupboards for even older family skeletons.

This much-enjoyed activity was a commonplace of Sunday afternoons in the music room of Kinburn Lodge. The music room was a large, dim apartment at the rear of the house, with a splendid view over the waste land and the betting men with their cards and their money.

The furnishings were faded, massive and gloomy. There was always a sort of hectic, suppressed air of whispered colloquy in the room, even when it was empty. I used sometimes to sit there alone, leafing through a 1930 *Chums* annual which was kept, for some unknown reason, perhaps even to keep me amused, among piles of sheet music in a glass-fronted, inlaid rosewood cabinet.

So far as I recall there was no piano in the room. The music was a relic. Sound was supplied nowadays by the raucous or subdued voices of my aunts and uncles, raised in dispute or lowered in innuendo, as they pursued the labyrinthine ins and outs of ancient feuds.

Nothing was ever forgotten; nothing, so far as I could see, ever forgiven. Heads were shaken in long-suffering sadness, hands lifted and let fall in expressive but silent hinting. Whoever was present was part of the fabric of denunciation, whoever was absent, its enveloped victim.

I would squat on a Moorish pouffe, or run my fingers over the raised felt ziggurats on the sides of the heavy armchairs, an unheard, and possibly even unseen, witness to these endlessly renewed wrangles and re-examined sources of grievance.

Even at a later date in my mid-teens I was never expected to interpose a comment or an opinion of my own, and I grew up with the reputation, quite false I think, for being a shy and quiet boy. I would much rather have taken part in the exercise of verbal diminishment, slaughtering reputations with a poniard in the back, and adding my own imaginative annexes to the crumbling outbuildings of traditional anecdotes.

It was not to be. I had sat through these afternoons too often, at too young an age, and I was always remembered, and even physically seen, I suppose, as a little boy from England, on holiday with his mother, quietly keeping himself to himself, and quite happy so long as he could get his nose in a book.

Alas, I would much rather have got my nose, like the rest of them, into a can of worms. It seemed more fun.

'I couldna forgive him, May,' a voice would say. 'I couldna forgive him, as long as I live.'

Long silences would intervene, broken perhaps by the rattle of teacups, or the low murmur of the word 'aye', the most popular and frequent interjection in these monologues.

'No,' the voice would continue, 'I couldna forgive him. Put yourself in ma position, May. Hoo could I forgive him? I couldna do it. I couldna do it, even if I wanted tae.'

My mother would shake her head, agreeing with this careful, reasonable judgement. Then the voice would resume, slow, meditative and bitter.

'If he walked in through that door the day, I couldna speak to him, May. After all he said to me, I couldna speak to him. No I couldna do it.'

Then perhaps another voice would chime in, adding its own grievous burden to the litany of blame.

'He was aye the same, Maggie. Aye the same. I mind once one time doon at Hughie's.'

Then a distant, unforgotten cause for reproach would be unearthed, like the corpse of a stillborn baby, from the fertile mulch of the past. The new voice would elaborate what everyone knew, and had heard renewed so often before.

'That's oor Jimmy' — or oor Davey, or oor Willie, or your Auntie Maggie, or your Auntie May — 'all over.'

Thus the voice would extract the general principle from the specific example, and the fugue of disapproval would gather momentum as other voices added their grace notes to the theme.

'They're all the same, the Kerrs'' — or the Manns or the Hutchisons — 'all the same. Aye, they're all the same.'

There would be a chorus of agreement at such a point as this, a modulating descant of brooding gloom.

'Aye, all the same. All the same.'

The truth of this last opinion, in retrospect, has struck me with much force. The taste for waspish, though sombre and melodic condemnation, ran like a strand of blood through the warp of every family encounter. But the drone of betrayal would exhaust itself, the searchlight of bitterness flicker at last in a blank void, and the compulsions of a more immediate hospitality regain their grip.

'Here, May, your cup's empty. Jimmy, give your Auntie May some more tea.'

So the afternoon would end, more amiably, with the refreshed rattle of cherished porcelain, the comfortable circulation of home-baked scones.

Back in Sheffield, the resonances of these hollow conversations would form a sonorous ground base for the more jerky, more openly abrasive dialogues of street and school. Oddly enough, the same word 'aye', though with a very different pronunciation, was one of the few common factors.

'He thwaarted me, though. Aye, he thwaarted me.'

Thus would some ancient sage of tea table or tram car be heard unburdening himself of a hoarded grouse against unknown colleague or awkward employer. The voice would be slow, rich, contemplative, savouring every vowel like a finger with a precious stone.

'Get that down thee.'

Thus would some second voice intervene, passing across a freshly toasted pikelet, or a glass of dandelion and burdock.

'Tha dun't want to have nought to do with him.'

So would this second voice, encapsulated maybe in the dandified person of Teddy Stokes, improve on hospitality with advice. Sheffield people were always very strong on advice.

'Tha wants to watch out, though. Tha'll get a clout in t'ear-oyle if tha dun't watch out.'

At school this biblical preservation of the old-fashioned second person singular tended to be ironed out, except in moments of anger or confrontation.

'Shut thy gob,' someone there would say.

After which, the flail of fists would replace the preliminary courtesies of Quaker English, and the bitten tongue or the blinded eye be forced to exclude either riposte or reprisal.

Meanwhile, the double dialogues in my head would murmur on, two streams of irreconcilable colloquy – the home Scots for my nightly conversations with my mother, tailored and spruced up to exclude the more violent or unseemly incidents of the day, and the school Yorkshire for the daily transactions with my scruffy peers.

I was still a boy of two voices, and I hoped I would never have to choose between them.

The struggle was sometimes hard.

14

Gang warfare at King Edward's had been developing in intensity. I seem to have risen, after my father's death, towards a position akin to the one held, albeit precariously, as successor to David Nelson at Greystones.

Perhaps the announcement of my father's death, which was the subject of a special prayer one morning, had marked me out as a figure uniquely afflicted by calamity, and thus well equipped to serve as the lightning conductor of revenge, the George Raft of the violence clique.

At any rate, I seem to have emerged at this date as the leader of a rather nasty gang. My main evidence for this is the memory of our dislocating a boy called Nicholson's back.

I don't know enough about anatomy to say whether this description of his injuries is an accurate one, but I recall it as the frightening — and no doubt intentionally ominous — phrase used by my headmaster to report what had happened.

Dr Barton was at once a severe and an inspiring man. He was the only master in the school invariably seen wearing a gown, and frequently a mortar board as well, so that he presented himself in the threatening regalia of office at all times, like a military policeman or general.

Indeed, he was very fond of military metaphor, and would exhort us from the platform at school assembly as members of a school 'of this calibre', as if the institution were a cannon of especially ferocious bore, aiming a series of destructive projectiles, ourselves, into a world of Nazi muddle and decay.

I rather enjoyed these harangues. They fitted in with my general picture of the world as a place of perpetual menace, and also as an arena for the display of heroic prowess.

Dr Barton's physiognomy was a great asset in his oratory. He had an eagle's hook of a nose, like the beak of a Viking ship, and his mouth below it was curved round and down into a supercilious, Roman smile. Thus the two traditions of

Western violence, the classical and the pagan, were effectively blended and given expression in his features.

He was not, however, a man who tolerated the outbreak of violence in any unlicensed form. You could hammer each other to death in the boxing ring, or, so far as the rules allowed, on the soccer field, but there was a strict, and strictly enforced, ban on playground fighting.

Thus do I see myself and my now forgotten lieutenants hauled before him in the affair of Nicholson and the allegedly damaged back. It was of no avail for us to claim, as we rightly and truly did, that Nicholson had wanted to become a member of our gang, and that we had only been submitting him to the normal tests for admittance.

These had included walking along the top of a narrow wall, and he had unfortunately, through no fault of ours, tumbled off, and landed awkwardly on his spine. We sympathised, and we were sorry for Nicholson, but we didn't see it as our fault.

The fact that Nicholson didn't either doesn't seem to have helped. The result was judged to be as bad as the process, though not necessarily worse. Dr Barton was keen not to allow any élite groups dominated by their own, and not the school's, ritual to interfere with his drive for general unity.

So we were punished, not mainly, I think, for damaging a boy's back, but more particularly for bucking the system, and setting up a loyalty focus external to the house structure. As we were still in the Junior School, the punishment was administered by the gym shoe and not the cane. For the only time in my experience, it was meted out by Dr Barton in person, and not by his delegate, Mr Baker.

This was clearly some indication of the gravity of our offence. As for Nicholson, I don't recall seeing him again. Alas, poor fellow, he probably suffered both from his damaged back and his sense of guilt, and his parents may have decided to remove him, when he recovered, from the fascinating penumbra of what had proved to be a dangerous violence.

Who knows? He perhaps became the leader of a brutal gang himself, and passed on the rituals of initiation to some other boy, in some other school, and thus had his revenge, though neither sought nor wanted, for the injury that was done to him.

Such things happen. Boys will be boys, and their ceremonies endure.

The most striking event at school, when I was ten, was the arrival of John Bingham. My earliest recollection is of a quiet, heavily built boy with dark black hair, who was exceptionally good at football.

In retrospect this ability at soccer seems rather surprising. Bingham's sporting future – and he was shortly always to be known to me either as Bingham or, more casually, simply as Ham – was to be as a cricketer, notably a batsman, famous for an obstinate defensive style which would resist all attempts at temptation.

Very shortly John Bingham became, and has thenceforward remained, my best friend. I was best man at his wedding, as he was best man at both of mine. I suppose I owe him one.

When we first met, his father had already volunteered, although over age, for army service, and was fighting somewhere abroad. I only met the older Bingham, a formidable man and a traveller in sherry, who had a rich Bristol-Cream voice and a massive frame like a barrel, when the war was over. He owned cinemas then and had houses inherited from his father.

Much later, when he died, I went up to Sheffield for his funeral and, arriving late at the church for the service, missed the fleet of cars going back to the family house. I was offered, and accepted, a lift in the hearse, the only time I shall travel in such a vehicle, I suppose, in my lifetime.

This kind of macabre experience, and the savouring of it, is perhaps something I share more closely with John Bingham than with anyone else. It springs, I suspect, from some peculiarly Yorkshire perverseness, which I imbibed with the choked factory air that still steams up from the River Don.

Enjoying disaster, and the bizarre manifestations of its occurrences, can make one seem callous, not to say brutally weird, or mad. We have both suffered from – or should I say been honoured by − such accusations. They bind, and they amuse.

At the time we first met I recall a different feature of the Bingham temperament, an odd nervousness, and public reticence. He would be slow to respond to the exchange of dirty jokes, for example, frowning silently down at his feet during the retailing of some coarsely exploitative schoolboy anecdote, such as the one about the naked girl who goes to a party as a wireless set.

First you twiddle the knobs, she said. But nothing's happening, the man replied. Oh, the girl said, but you've forgotten to plug in. Forgotten to plug in, get? And so, it seemed, had our new football star, John Bingham, who was too shy, or too prudish, to see this as funny, or worth laughing at.

Looking back, one respects his good taste. But this could be carried sometimes to absurd extremes. In the course of almost any conversation in a public place, even on the most innocuous subjects, he would lean close, look surreptitiously to either side, and then lower his voice to a ludicrously confidential whisper, of a kind I often thought − and in fact still do − likely to attract rather than deter attention by its very parody of privacy.

Nevertheless, this unusual boy had a will of steel. He could hypnotise himself to avoid feeling pain at the dentist's, and I saw him prove this once by holding a lighted match to the palm of his hand, until the flesh charred.

One day I shall go back to Shotts, where I was born. I read once in some magazine that it has the finest miner's swimming pool in Scotland. I should like to see that. I suppose, though, that my failure to return, over all the years, has been out of a sense that the past can never be recaptured.

The Shotts I want to see, the dream Shotts where I pushed my toy wheelbarrow under a sky dark with bursting shells, and where my dog Mac lay at my feet like Cerberus before the king of Hell, this has gone forever, if indeed it ever existed.

I know it only from photographs. Mac, in particular − the black Labrador who looks up expectantly so often from under the basket chair where the baby in the fur hat sleeps below his parasol – even Mac is only an image, not a memory, though I rack my brains to try and lift him back from the well of time.

Shotts was an aptly named place for Mac to live. He looked after me for the first six months of my life, and then was shot one day for chasing sheep. His death seems to launch me already, months before proper consciousness, into the world stream of violence.

I must have been deeply affected, at some subterranean level, by the death of this devoted creature. I always feel close to animals and, however sad I may feel, the sight of an animal can always lift my spirits and make life seem worth living. I remember warming even to Hitler, when I heard how he had brought up a young Alsatian with his own hands.

In my more belligerent moments I have been heard to declare that I prefer animals to people, and see no reason to regard them as inferior. This is never a popular opinion, and is usually treated as a joke.

It would be so treated, I fear, by John Bingham, with whom I once presided over what he called a froggy Belsen, bombarding a mass of small, green, webby beasts in a pool with a handful of stones. Boys are a mess of inconsistencies, and love and cruelty lie close together.

I entered the Senior School in 1943. Entered, in fact, as we junior inmates always did, by a plain pair of glazed green doors on the ground floor. The broad flight of steps, flanked by grooved urns, which led up under Corinthian capitals to a sumptuous portico, was reserved for masters, and for adult visitors.

The school was – and remains, to be fair, in its Comprehensive form – a distinguished Edwardian–Roman building, built of dressed stone, a little soot-blackened, as is fitting for a great industrial city, and facing a wide lawn behind a circling stone wall.

The Junior School, long since closed, was only a short walk away, and I was quite familiar with the surroundings of the main building, which I had visited regularly for swimming periods. These were conducted in the indoor pool, housed near the lower gates, redolent of chlorine, and echoing with voices and splashing.

The interior of the main building had remained something of a mystery. Now the whole truth was revealed, a layered secrecy of corridors and classrooms, ranked in rows, floor above floor, and focusing from all points on the central Assembly Hall.

A sweeping balcony, like the upper range of a Methodist church, curled round above rows of stained pine benches, and looked down on an apron platform, with a brass lectern, where an eagle supported an open Bible.

From here, each morning, one of the prefects would read out some improving message, concluding with a traditional *Here endeth the lesson*. It must be a mark of my own ingenuity as well as my wickedness, that I altered the phrasing on one notorious occasion to: *And may the Lord add His blessing to this reading of His Holy Word*, which was what we usually said at St Andrew's on Sundays.

The change was not approved, though it was difficult, as I had seen it would be, to construe the alteration as insolence. Thus did low cunning sometimes succeed in cocking a snook at the system.

More honest rebellion, such as that of my friend Dawson, an anarchic and civilised boy, who wanted to be a film director, and once refused to stand up for the singing of 'God Save the King', was brutally suppressed. I suspect that lack of patriotism was ranked as a worse vice than blasphemy.

In 1943 I had few opportunities to exhibit revolutionary tendencies and, besides, I was anxious to conform. I wanted to gain credit with older colleagues in what was a dauntingly new and indifferent world.

So I sat quietly in my lowly place near to the back of the balcony and looked down in awe at the glass cases where each of the eight school houses had a baize-lined cupboard for the display of athletic trophies. I vowed that I would struggle to see that my own house improved its show of silver.

The houses were all named after grand houses, great Yorkshire or Derbyshire mansions such as Chatsworth and Haddon, Wentworth and Arundel. My own Lynwood was one of the less well-known, though I didn't know that at the time. I only heard the name as a high, forlorn, fleeting call from the touchline of some muddy pitch, where a rain-soaked eleven in striped blue shirts were battling for an elusive victory.

Many would still be battling, and some dying, only a few months later, when they left school for the Western Desert, or the North Atlantic Convoys, or the waste airfields of East Anglia, and the wide skies above the English Channel.

Perhaps, after all, there was a real point in Dr Barton seeing King Edward's in those years as a school with a calibre. What else were we being trained for except to fight and die?

15

The war, as it developed, brought its own appropriate pursuits, even for those of us too young as yet to foresee conscription. One of the more universal of these was an interest in aircraft recognition.

The Observer Corps, which fostered this, had been formed fairly early in the war, and had done useful service in correctly identifying enemy bombers, which was not, in fact, so easy as one might suppose.

I believe that the first aeroplane shot down in 1939 was one of our own fighters, a Hurricane which had been scrambled in response to a warning of bandits approaching, and had then been attacked by another squadron, airborne slightly later, and supposing that it had overtaken a raider.

Needless to say, this ironic, and rather horrifying, story was not known at the time. It doesn't, in fact – and not surprisingly perhaps, in view of the circumstances of my father's death – strike me that this will have been a unique incident. Mistakes are part of the texture of war.

It was an attempt to unravel some part of this misleading texture that led to the widespread interest in the many small handbooks, and the specialist magazine *The Aeroplane Spotter*, that served as aids to correct identification.

I adored these handbooks. At the age of twelve I saved up twelve and sixpence for a portly little volume known as a dumpy book, which included silhouettes and specifications of all the known aeroplanes in the world.

My pre-war, 1936 Jane's was out of date, but it provided some useful background, as well as establishing high standards of detail. Pressures of censorship withheld much information, such as the top speeds of new fighters, and this was avidly sought by small boys, just as it no doubt was by elderly foreign air marshals, and enemy spies, on both sides.

There was even one curious paperback which included a series of Oddentifications, caricature drawings which overemphasised the main features of aeroplanes, and thus made them easier to pick out. There were short rhymes, too, which put these originalities into words.

I still own my Oddentifications book, a tattered remnant with a yellow cover and a gambolling flying boat on it. The slimmer, darker volumes of my Aircraft Recognition diaries lie cheek by jowl in a drawer, and my bound volumes – alas, all post-war ones – of the revered *Aeroplane Spotter* are stored in a suitcase.

In actual practice, one rarely had the opportunity to try out one's skill. Aeroplanes were, for me, the opposite on the whole of what children were supposed to be. They were heard, but not seen.

I would lie awake night after night as the war wore on and listen to the British bombers droning overhead on their way to Cologne or Dresden: an inexorable, grinding roar of power, the slowly applied vengeance of the roused lion against those who had so unwisely twisted its tail in 1940.

Nowadays there is much criticism of the Allied night bombing offensive against civilian targets, and some argument that it was ineffective as well as inhumane. I can understand this. But those, like me, who have stepped out of the ruins of their own homes into searchlights and shrapnel can perhaps be excused for having listened to the nightly whine of Trenchard's axe with a sense of righteous pride.

By 1944, rationing had become tougher, and more organised. A points system was introduced, whereby luxury – or supposedly luxury – items such as tinned salmon and South African snoek could be obtained upon the surrender of a certain number of coupons.

There were grades of salmon, and even the lowest one, presumably sections near to the head or tail, required a substantial allowance of points. Bread, at one period, was on the ration, and I believe that there was a question of it being joined there by potatoes.

Not all retailers were diligent in their support of these measures. In Scotland, to my certain knowledge, the system of bread rationing was never universally implemented.

Nor, indeed, was the ban on the manufacture of ice-cream. The enterprising Italian vendors in Hamilton — Tony on one side of the road and Peter Ecchi on the other — simply altered the name of their produce from ice-cream to snow-freeze, and continued to manufacture it with impunity and profit.

At the very end of the war, no doubt as evidence of how effectively our Britannic navy had re-assumed the rule of the waves, a small number of mildly exotic fruits began to reappear. Bananas, for example, were available for very young children.

In 1945 I saw an example of how scarcity could be made consistent with the avoidance of grievance, at any rate in a capitalist society familiar with the laws of supply and demand. A single peach was offered for sale in a Hamilton shop window at twenty-four shillings.

One pound twenty pence would be a high price for a single peach today, I imagine. Something like fifteen times this price was one of the concomitants of total, as we were now taught to call it, war.

Unconditional surrender was what was expected of the German forces, unlike the qualified throwing in of the towel allowed the Italians, who, after all, had been our allies in the First World War, and were, anyway, never taken very seriously by British propaganda.

There were stories of Italian regiments retreating so fast in the desert that they left their boots behind. There were no stories which pointed out that some of these Italian soldiers came from families so poor that they had probably never worn boots even in peacetime. After the war was over, I used to see children in a similar situation in the streets of Glasgow.

With unconditional surrender the fate for the die-hard Nazis, I spent the early months of 1944 pasting maps of the Normandy landings and the Falaise Gap into a blue notebook, as I strove to follow the strategy of our advancing generals.

On the other side of Europe, no doubt small boys in Russia were doing the same sort of thing, as the Red Army broke the panzer divisions on the great plains in front of Kiev. The empire that was to last 1,000 years was in the pincers of a terrible movement, gripped and crushed as securely from

both sides as the planks of wood I had seen my father place in
the steel jaws of the metal vice in his tool-shed.

What my father left me was a chain of memories, though
most of them have shredded out and thinned away like clouds
in a wind. I have one which remains, more obstinate, and
unsupported by any photographic gloss or anecdotal
summary.

My father is walking beside me, taking me to school along
Clarkehouse Road, and he is holding my hand. He wears, and
this is the most incongruous element in the memory, a heavy,
double-breasted, worsted overcoat.

I don't recall this overcoat in any other situation except the
context of this one memory. My father no doubt left behind a
large number of clothes, which my mother presumably gave
away, either to relatives or to charities. I certainly don't
remember a stock of them still hung in the wardrobes.

Only a few items were retained for my own later use. The
spats my father wore for his wedding re-emerged in my
courting days at Oxford, and were accompanied by a double-
breasted waistcoat, a wedding grey tie, and a tightly rolled
umbrella.

The Freudian perfection of this Oedipal get-up – the young
suitor both literally and symbolically garbed in the robes and
with the sceptre of his lord and father – only became apparent
to me much later, and under therapy.

At the time, the spats – grey-silver, and with little pearl
buttons down the sides – were the subject of a short satirical
poem in *terza rima*, printed in the *Isis*. I was flattered by this,
though pretending a sense of outrage.

The spats, alas, wore out, and I no longer have them. So
did my father's driving gloves – in fact, a pair of gargantuan
leather-backed mittens, with a fur fabric interior – which I
put on to keep my hands warm in exceptionally cold
weather.

I remember these mittens with affection. They had a
tawdry, much rubbed surface, and were always bursting at
the seams, to emit a peeking fragment of greasy orange wool.
My mother, knowing how much I liked them, and perhaps

sharing this affection herself, would sew the false fur back in, and the mittens would enjoy a fresh lease of life.

Perhaps my father, too, seemed to enjoy some fresh lease of life in these post-mortem travels of his massive gloves. They were far too big for my tiny hands, but this very bigness enabled my fingers to move freely, and thus avoid becoming numb.

Somehow the mittens followed the spats into oblivion. There must have come a day when they were too ragged even for my mother to find a way of renewing their youth with her magic needle. The past lurched one step further away, and the mittens became the substance only of recollection, extracted and discarded from the jumble of forgotten scarves and worn tennis balls in the bottom of our walnut hall stand.

Now the only surviving item of my father's clothing is a 1930s dressing-gown, patterned with interlocking black and rust ziggurats, like a series of imaginary Aztec temples designed by M. C. Escher. Frayed though it is, with braided cording around the pockets that has begun to come loose, and a certain lack of shine and glaze in the tassels which tip the belt for tying at the waist, it nevertheless exudes an aura of exotic cocktails in tall glasses, or idle mornings on the decks of ocean-going yachts.

These occasions hardly fit the image of my father as he emerges at home or at work. But they serve to add an extra tone to his background, the razzmatazz of the jazz age, with its fast cars, fast women, and slow tangos.

When I wear the dressing-gown, which is rarely, fearful as I am of doing it some irreparable damage, it seems to hang, to quote my namesake play, like a giant's robe upon a dwarfish thief. I seem to have returned to the age when I wore the enormous driving mittens, and to be far too small, too inadequate somehow, for the dressing-gown to fit.

I still wonder, though, about that incongruous memory of my father walking with me, in his heavy overcoat. The overcoat seems, the more I think of it, to grow more and more like the dressing gown. So that finally I come to wonder if, here too, there is no reality in the outward form of the memory, but only a will to create some ineradicably close connection, a worn garment which still hangs in my own mahogany bedroom wardrobe, and which I can reach down, and be enveloped by, whenever I choose.

Curiously enough, the memory of my father walking there in Clarkehouse Road is the last memory I have of him. There is none later. I clutch his hand. Father, I want to say. And suddenly reality has drifted across an invisible line, where there is no solace left, except a deifying abstraction. My father is about to become, like the emperor Hadrian – alas – a god.

The influence of Latin on my thinking was already quite strong by the time I was eleven. I had read some of Caesar's commentaries, and a speech or two by Cicero, and one or two books of the *Aeneid*. Helpful books such as *Everyday Life in Ancient Rome*, backed up by Arthur Mee's *Children's Encyclo-paedia*, of which I had a forbidding navy blue set in my bedroom, helped to build up some picture of how the Roman soldiers and the Trojan exiles lived when they were at home.

The pagan virtue of stoicism, as displayed in such figures as the elder Cato or, more dashingly, the noble Horatius who kept the bridge in Lord Macauley's poem, was visibly high-lighted in whatever texts we had to hand.

The Romans appeared to have been very much like we modern Britons, the unwilling but responsible managers of a vast and unruly empire and one threatened from time to time, like our own, by the madness of Africans, Jews or Huns. I don't think this was ever spelled out, certainly not by the tactful and energetic Jean Knight, but it nevertheless leaked into our brains from a hundred epigrams, and another hundred or more verses, legends, and myths.

Our studied periods were the later Republic and the early Empire, so that the excesses of primitive savages, and the later orgies of decadent sophisticates, were alike shrouded from view. I never realised, for example, what gross models of splendour and decay were offered by such figures as Domitian and Messalina. As for Heliogabalus, after a completed classical education, and a degree supposedly qualifying me as a reasonable initiate in Roman history, I still know him only from conversation.

Someone once told me that he was killed by being pushed

head first down a lavatory, but this was not the kind of detail that was ever pressed on my attention at King Edward VII School. It might, after all, have put the wrong sort of ideas in our heads.

Romans tended to be heroes, patricians and men. Their slaves, their tiny-breasted whores and their priapic deities were kept well out of sight. Ovid was bowdlerised, Martial was left in Latin, or, if translated, versified in Italian. An English gentleman might know just enough French, or conceivably even German, to snuffle up some corruption, but the language of Casanova would surely put the poison out of his reach.

Greek, when it came, was a source of annoyance. We had a system at King Edward's whereby a third language − after Latin and French − was usually commenced upon entry to the Senior School. The choices in my day were Greek, German or Spanish.

German was already tainted as the language of the devil. I can still hardly hear its guttural expletives without associating them with wartime propaganda. German remains the tongue of schoolboy comics and second feature films, where cardboard Nazis exclaim *Donner und Blitzen* as the oil-wells blow up, or hammer the table to explain that something is *verboten*, or scream *Achtung!* as they race for their motor cycles.

German, therefore, was ruled out. My own strong preference was for Spanish, largely, I think, because I had seen what a large area of the globe, very notably almost the whole of South America, consisted of former Spanish colonies. The imperial spirit was strong.

Dr Barton, however, advised my mother that I would be sensible to take Greek. My Latin was good, and the combination of both languages would enable me to compete for classical scholarships at Oxford and Cambridge.

This was perfectly true, and it was wise advice, but I resented the interference with my own freedom of choice, and I commenced my Greek studies with suppressed rage.

I now think that a classical education, though long placed on the back-burner of my intellectual gas cooker, is something I would be very sorry to have been without. It took time to see its advantages, and its day-by-day pleasures, in the years of mastering the languages, were few.

I slaved over dictionaries too heavy to lift, I filled thin blue books with vocabularies of epithets and cases, I wrote in my sleazy copperplate ingenious interpretations of rare battles. Latin and Greek began to be synonymous, quite simply, with work.

It was the business of refining meaning – either in translation or composition – that filled our days. The interest of the great works we handled as literature was disguised, obliterated – almost, so it seemed, derided – in this process.

And yet something, gradually, seeped through. I began to admire the mute, searing extremities of Greek tragedy, the concentration camp of the mind. I could see the Greeks on the plains of Troy in the same terms as the armoured divisions in their assault on Monte Cassino.

Later I would think of Hector, saying goodbye to his wife and his little son, before he went out to fight Achilles, knowing that he had no chance of winning, but going out all the same. This seemed to me the central ikon of what heroism should be. After all, in the stripped outline of my private mythology, it was exactly what my father had done. Hector was his precedent, his legendary forebear.

But it took my adolescence, and later Oxford, to learn this.

By the end of 1944, I was entirely absorbed in a world of sport. I was fighting to win a place in the soccer under-fourteen eleven, and I had become a dour cross-country runner. The one Greek writer most likely to have appealed to me, though then left unread as being too difficult, was Pindar, with his paeans of praise to the athletes at the Olympic games.

Our own Olympic games, in their fervour and their envy, were enacted on the muddy arena of Furness Fields, a sloping hill on the outskirts of Sheffield, reached by a bus journey followed by a walk through woods of chestnut and elm.

Cross-country, a savage practice involving miles of hard slog through ploughland and over stiles, up hill and down valley, allowed us the run, literally, of a broad stretch of various countryside. In good weather, and with no spirit of competition, the runs might have been a pleasant way of seeing our Yorkshire outdoors.

In pelting rain, and bitter wind, they tended to offer an exhausting, if a salutary, means of scourging the flesh and the will. I used to run in plimsoles, play soccer in studded boots. Either way, the changing in and out of this footwear, and its accompanying washing and ribaldry, took place in what was always called the Pavilion.

The Pavilion came into its own in summer when it was indeed a pavilion, and sold orange drinks and snowballs. It then allowed an idle gaggle of stumped or caught batsmen to view the surrounding wickets.

In autumn and winter, I recall the Pavilion as a draughty box, icy cold, except in the whistling showers, from which naked elves would emerge with flicking towels, howling like dervishes and about as dirty as when they went in. On particularly ill-disciplined occasions, a disliked boy might have handfuls of wet mud stuffed down his football knickers while he was busy dubbing his boots.

The object was to work as much of this filthy substance as possible into the freshly showered crannies of his testicles and, to this end, his arms and legs were pinned, and his yelps ignored. Other pursuits would include jumping on to the back of some prone or bending youth and grunting ferociously in the manner of a rutting boar, while accompanying this soundtrack with suitably flamboyant visuals in the form of thrusting and squirming motions.

I realise that, although we never got further than this, it may seem that I am adding, in spite of my previous disclaimer, an additional episode to the extended one of the pilling epidemic, which I have claimed was unique. It may be so. Do I contradict myself? as Whitman said. Very well then I contradict myself.

However, I incline to see these Pavilion cavortings as no more than juvenile horseplay, as devoid of sexual content as the statuesque posings and posturings on the soccer pitches, which they grotesquely succeeded, and to which they formed a somewhat lewd, though inoffensive, coda.

Not so inoffensive the games and the running themselves. It was soon to be apparent that an overcasual attitude to the business of wrapping up warmly, and to taking hot showers, could lead to dangerous physical illness.

16

One morning in December 1944 I woke up with severe pains in my legs. I told my mother, and she suggested that I stay at home, and see how I felt. I was allowed to come downstairs, and to lie on the settee in the sitting-room, but I didn't want much to sit up, or to read.

I had a high fever, and there was a rapid pulsing in my wrists. My mother took my temperature in the evening and was sufficiently shocked, by what she saw on the thermometer, to call the doctor in. I lay alone on the settee while she went round the corner to fetch him.

The pains were worse, and unlike anything I had experienced before. I can't envisage what to compare them with, but I can remember how bad they were. I suppose I was quite frightened by this, but I had faith in the doctor, and waited reasonably patiently.

Dr MacIntyre was a neat, serious little Scotsman, in his mid-fifties. He had a slow voice, a three-piece suit, and a stethoscope.

He took my temperature, then my pulse. He looked at my legs. He sounded my chest and my heart. Then he pronounced that I probably had some germ, and that I'd better stay in bed for a day or two.

A germ in those days was about as vague and as threatening an entity as a German. It allowed an avoidance of any specific attribution of dangers or propensities, while indicating a need to be careful and combat ill effects, as soon as possible, by some massive counter-attack.

In Dr MacIntyre's case, this took the form of a dose of aspirins. Excellent though this willow remedy can be, it had more or less no effect – either on my pain, or on my fever. I spent the night in intervals of delirium broken by painful wakefulness, and it was apparent to my anxious mother that the doctor would have to be called again in the morning.

By now the pains were worse, and seemed to be all over my

body. Dr MacIntyre returned, sounded me again, took my pulse and decided that I had better go into hospital for observation. An ambulance was called, an entirely new vehicle in my life, and with excitement mounting, and a touch of fear glittering in the midst of what was mainly, I think, a sense of pride at being the centre of attention, I was whisked away to the Royal Hospital.

As soon as they got me there, they realised I had rheumatic fever.

In the 1940s rheumatic fever was the sort of disease you died of. Modern medicine has made it fairly easy to combat, but this was not so at the end of the war. While the Allied armies were advancing across the German frontier, and Hitler was mounting his final counter-offensive in the Ardennes, I was fighting for my life in the Royal Hospital.

I was put in a ward where I was the youngest inhabitant. The next youngest was a boy of fourteen, suffering, I think, from kidney trouble, who used to sit up in bed in a waistcoat. He was the first character I knew in real life who dressed strikingly in what has come to be a leitmotif of my story. But, like Jesse James, he too died; shot, as it were, in the back.

The screens moved, and someone else came to fill the bed. In the three weeks I was there, from mid-December, over Christmas and into the New Year, the folding screens were a perpetual reminder of mortality and pain. Their flowered material, ruched like a woman's knickers, offered a coy shelter for the brute finalities of torment, the polished cauldron of extinction.

Sometimes, the screens came only with the bedpan, but even then they might mask a terrible straining, an agony of frustrated retention, the costive preliminary to a humiliating visit by a nurse with a rubber tube and a bowl of soapy water. I endured constipation and then enemas myself, and they were never pleasant.

Neither these, however, nor the enshrouded colloquies while starched sisters applied iron bars to my calves and forearms, and attached me, like an American gangster about to die in the electric chair, to a machine which would monitor the beat of my heart, were in the same, final, horrific realm of grimness as the scorching unbandaging sessions, when others fresh from operating theatre or casualty ward would have lint or linen stripped from their naked wounds.

Yells were infrequent. The English dislike yelling. But the nights, under the dim blue of the nurse's reading lamp, were punctuated by an orchestrated medley of groans. Asleep, or dozing, men in pain found it harder to maintain that famous stiff upper lip of which we were all so proud.

I would lie in this cavern of echoing darkness awake and sweating, and then shortly awake and cold, and then finally half-asleep and riven by an underworld of nightmare and vague expectation of evil. My pains, bad as they had been, were curiously quick to disappear, which makes me think that the crisis of my illness had passed by the time Dr MacIntyre sent me into hospital.

I was fevered, and frightened, but hardly what I myself would have called ill any more. Nevertheless, I was made to be ill, whether I wanted to be or not: a small Czech doctor came to see me one day, and sat on the edge of the bed, and gave me the sort of news that hit an active boy of twelve like a promise of death.

You won't be able to play games for a while, he said, serious and foreign.

I was no fool. I knew what he meant. From that day on my foot would never touch a football again. I was a broken athlete, as useless to my house or school as the willow of a cricket bat with a split in the grain.

Hearing the news of my retirement, and lying in a ward where so many people died, I began gradually, as I got better, to realise how ill I must have been. I was told, for example, that I had to lie flat on my back, with no pillows, because there was a weakness in my heart, and I had to avoid all form of strain.

So I lay looking at the ceiling, or twisting my head sideways to ruin my eyes by reading a book wrenched awkwardly askew, or trying to drink over-milky tea from a little cup with a spout, like a teapot.

The slow days wore by. The ward was decorated for Christmas, with gaudy streamers and unfolding accordion-like bells, and in due course Santa Claus came round with a bag of presents, and made affable jokes, and did nothing to reduce the anguish of being away from home.

People were always coming round. There were the regular doctors' visits every morning and evening, when my temperature chart — an evenish red line now, instead of a mountain range of awesome peaks and troughs — would be lifted, flicked over and approved.

Then there would be the kitchen staff with food, an appalling wartime sludge far below the standards of what I was used to. I ate little, except for slices of bread with margarine. This seems to have been thought an appropriate consequence of my fever, and no one seemed to mind.

When Toc H would come, a nice man with a tray of reading matter around his neck, I would select as many books as I was allowed. I began to read more seriously than at home, and made the acquaintance of *Tarka the Otter* and *Salar the Salmon*. The extremes of these creatures' lives felt in harmony with my own.

One of the nicer features of my hospitalisation was a realisation that I was still within the orbit of my father's care. The staff of his office, remembering what he had done, clubbed together and raised some money to buy me a group of expensive books.

They were a thoughtful, intelligent choice, and I have them still. Some were too old for me, like the *History of Everyday Things in England 1733–1875*, with its fascinating photographs of steam engines and stoves. Others, such as *Brendan Chase*, provided an image of the England, or the English countryside, for which I suppose our armies were fighting. It matched the rather right-wing animal stories of Henry Williamson. I read *Brendan Chase* with careful avidity. It told me, among other things, that thatching was about to become extinct.

Mercifully, it hasn't. Like so many predictions of the gloomy 1940s, this woeful notion was proved wrong. The counter-offensive in the Ardennes was broken, the advance on Berlin continued, and the war came to an end, with soldiers dancing in the streets, and confetti flung in the air like bitter almonds.

But the war is never over. I realised that already one day as I lay and looked across the ward to where a thin, wasted man was gasping for breath on his pillow. He didn't gasp for long. The nurses came, and then, rolling on silent rubber wheels along the linoleumed floor of the ward, like the fuselage of a military aeroplane, the wingless, terrifying yellow canister of an iron lung.

I watched the man for hours inside the iron lung. All day it stood on its wheeled base, replacing his bed. And at night it poked its flattened nose out from the shallow ellipses of folded screens, like a German bomber emerging from its hangar.

In the morning, when I woke for breakfast, the iron lung had been taken away and a new, more healthy-looking face stared across at me from a freshly made bed. The iron lung had arrived as a saviour, but its fortress walls had been penetrated by the enemy in the night. The wasted man who had gasped for breath had gone for ever.

Later, when I read the Victorian poet Eugene Lee-Hamilton, I was struck by his perception that those who die in hospital are like soldiers who fall in the front line, dying in the face of a common enemy. This was not so much in Lee-Hamilton's case an insight as an apology, since he spent nearly twenty years of his own life supine on a wheeled stretcher, suffering from what his biographers have called a dread cerebrospinal complaint.

Nevertheless, the analogy is a consoling one. In wartime, if I had known it, it might have consoled me. We were all at war, and it would have been nice to think of those of us in hospital as doing our bit.

The Terminus

Last night I dreamed you came back. In my cot
Of cane I kicked, squat fingers curled like ferns
    Around your beads. I was just one
And needed things to clutch. Too late one learns
    (Love passing) all we miss in what
We reach to hold. This morning, in the sun

Along that crowded street, I walked and saw
The ether clear, and your keen face etched through
    As if on glass. Under the glaze
Of pre-war Kodak in my blood-book, you
    (As in my mind's eye) pose and thaw
Before my father's hands. In furs you laze

Beside his 30s car with filled-in wheels
While picnic-baskets open. You drink tea
    On grass. Then by a rock you stand
Staring at sepia water. And with me
    In tow, throw bread to leaping seals
(That must be Glasgow) smiling. Sun and sand

Open their honeyed vistas, and the war
Swims under water, years away. I turn
    Pages of pity. Here I sit
With Mac who licked my face when I was born
    And died for worrying sheep. A door
Into my father's death parts. Here you knit

A fair-isle jersey for him, here link arms
With arms in khaki, here take off his hat
    And kiss his thin hair. Were you pleased
In this one where you seem to laugh and chat
    As he drives off? And what alarms
You in this weirdly blurred one? Were you seized

By fear or simply dazzled? There's no end
To all they hint. Each thick page in my brain
    Erupts and bleeds. Rich blood of kin,
Dense with the war, wells upwards like a stain
    Through all my strange thoughts. And no bend
In sleep or waking movement folds it in

Or stops him dying. Blood is in my veins
From things that happened in your body where
    His cool hands touched it, where I lay
Before my birth. In you I climbed a stair
    Whose treads were water, wearing chains
Of ropes of flesh that I was free to fray,

Though not to break. And when my birth day came
I could swing out. And there in light I broke
    And stood bare-naked. I was king
Of all the flowers and sunlight by one stroke
    Of silver blades. I owned his name
And both your blood. Tonight on blood I bring

My anchored body from his broken back
To your thrown side. I count the standing men
    And watch their whispers. Through the door
I hear you weeping. Someone sees me. Then
    They take me in. I sense the crack
In our closed wall and cry for you. Then your

Own time is here. I come to your pale side
And enter in. So many miles of stone
    After that sea I have to walk
Before I reach you! Why is your clean bone
    So bare? Has the receding tide
Sucked all your living tissue, left me chalk

Where nothing grows? No brilliant cells I see,
No poison dew. Death's music plays in green
    On inner ground so often. Growth
Lush as below the sea. Not here. No sheen
    Of dense bloom gathers. That would be
Some bright relief from this blue stone. On both

Sides of your body I confront chalk, find
Only the barren, scentless, tasteless rock
    Of your dry death. So I return
(Dreams passing into day) through glass. I lock
    Your stone wood in my inward mind
And come alive. I feel hot coffee burn,

Laving my throat. I lie on green brocade
Stretched over cane, reflecting. Fifteen hours
    It is since I was in that sleep
Where you were living still. Do any flowers
    Bloom on your grave? I hear a spade
Grate over clay. Years later, I can weep

Only for your belongings: a green jar,
A crocodile-skin hand-bag, a long brush
    That touched your hair. I hold it here
And scrape some living tissue. I could rush
    To tears. I think bereaved men are
Too far at sea in grief for this. How clear

In blood of mind can I be, losing love
At such a distance? Here above your hair
    I know the way to learn. I lie
Broad waking on my cool bed. I am bare
    As he was with you. High above
On this first night I feel wind stroke the sky

And stir my skin. Close by I hear the tune
Of falling rain. And when your body comes
    In gauze like sea-mist from the shore
At morning, I put out my sails from slums
    To clean sea. And below the moon
I enter you in joy, as none before.

17

The treatment I was given for my fever seems to have been minimal. It amounted, in fact, to no more than rest, aspirins, and a strange, sickly-bitter liquid served from a tall bottle in twice-daily doses of a tablespoonful at a time.

Whether these medicines were effective, or whether my body simply got on with ameliorating my condition on its own, I don't know, but I did improve; sufficiently, at any rate, to be shifted from the Royal Hospital to a convalescent home on the outskirts of the city.

There, in a bright, sun-catching ward with a long verandah where tubercular patients could be put out for air, I languished for a further five months, feeling perfectly well, and desperate to be free. I was allowed to sit up, but not to get out of bed, and the date of my eventual release remained uncertain.

My mother came to see me, as she was allowed to, only twice a week, and I longed for these visits as a prisoner with a life sentence might long for the brief weekly sight of his wife and children. She brought me sweets, and things to read, and I think little delicacies to improve my teas.

Life was so unvaried in the hospital, and I felt so deprived of affection, that I would look forward to the chance of being given one particular white mug, which was shorter and more chunky and huggable, to my eye, than the others.

I stored up the details of how many times I had been lucky enough to get this cup, and my mother would be bored with an account of these. The details remain, in smudgy script, written down in the pocket diary I kept for the first part of 1945.

There were other, more dramatic incidents. But it was the loss of love, the sense of needing a larger ration of affectionate attention, that stays most vividly in mind.

A man with a hernia at the far end of the ward seemed to be a great favourite with the younger girls, and he led a flirtatious and giggly life of teasing and innuendo, from which I felt vaguely excluded. Older men would often be laughing at remarks or incidents whose meaning was obscure to me.

Indeed, I was quite unaware, until he was moved for some too overt observation or gesture to another ward, that the friendly man in the adjacent bed to mine had been thought to be taking a sexual interest in me, culminating, I believe, in an attentive monologue while viewing my back being rubbed by a nurse with oil to alleviate bedsores.

The successor to this dirty fellow was in time found equally wanting, though for another reason. This new patient was a tramp, and he had nothing wrong with him. Every winter, he would manage to get himself into hospital on the pretext of some ailment which would ensure him board and lodging through the coldest weather.

I spent hours listening to his stories of extortion. He obviously liked me, albeit in a less physical way, because when he was discharged he came to see me with a present of a book.

I was touched by his thoughtfulness, knowing how little money he had. Alas, I was not allowed to keep the book. It had been stolen from a patient in the ward next door.

At last, what had seemed to be inconceivable, happened. I was allowed to go home. The war had ended while I was in hospital, and I came out into a world at peace. The daffodils had bloomed and gone, the cherry was in blossom, and the sun was shining.

But it was only the war in Europe that was over. The Japanese were still fighting – as, or so I have been told, they would be fighting now unless the emperor had told them to stop – and the celebrations for VJ Day were still two months away.

The atomic bomb, whose resonance was to be so colossal in the 1960s, made little impact at the time, at any rate on my own preoccupation with learning how to walk, an art which had faded in the drear months of embedded nursing.

I well remember how astonished I was to set feet on the ground and feel that they wouldn't support me. I had supposed that the strength in my legs would be ready to well up, and shine forth, like electric light at the touch of a switch. It wasn't. It took me many days to resume a normal walking life.

As for my former life of running and football, that was never to be resumed. One day, six years ahead, after unending requests, the ageing Dr MacIntyre, himself now a prey to heart disease, would agree that my valvular condition had improved to the point where I could play games again, and I would strip and go into practice, jogging round and round the school close like a slow rabbit.

I entered the quarter-mile in the summer games, a distance I had once been a champion at. There were many, no doubt, who felt proud to see this ancient war-horse emerging again, as it were from the knacker's yard, but the years had been too many, and the muscles refused to work. I collapsed after 200 yards, in front but finished.

Thus ended my athletic career, save for a brief final flicker at the table-tennis table, where I continued to achieve some feats of distinction even at Oxford, playing once for my college.

The defeat of the supposed heart weakness has been a lifelong challenge. I was delighted once in my mid-twenties, after climbing Mount Parnassus, and then walking over twenty miles back to our hotel, to rise the following morning and find my rugby-playing companion-climber flat on his back and then hobbling on a stick, while I was fit enough to go out and visit the site of Delphi unaided.

This kind of self-satisfaction, shading into petty boastfulness, is one of the less attractive concomitants of being, or having been, an invalid. The urge to 'prove it' is a strong one, and the temptation to point out that it has been proved can be even stronger.

At the age of thirteen, unlucky thirteen, in the choppy wake of fever, there was little opportunity to be proving anything. I kept having recurrences of high temperature, with an increased pulse rate, and was often ordered to return to bed, although not, mercifully, to hospital.

The fear was always of a full return of the fever, which was prone to damage the heart even more irretrievably at its second go. Very few people, I believe, survived a third bout. So whatever minor ailment smote me, and set my heart racing, the cautious Dr MacIntyre would have me confined to bed.

There I would lie, bored, outraged, and humiliated. Not only was I prevented from playing games, I was even stopped from breasting the tape first in the class. It was probably this frustrated athlete's irritation more than anything else which led me to look for some extra-curricular field of endeavour in which to excel.

What I came up with – rather surprisingly – was writing prose.

My school had a Cinema Club, recently formed, and it now publicised a competition for a script, which would in due course be made into a film. I seized this opportunity with gusto. I wrote, from my bed, and entered, still from my bed, what I believed would be a certain winner.

It wasn't. But it was something much more important. It was the means of my realising that I actually enjoyed writing. From then on, whenever I was ill again, I would while away the crawling hours by taking out an exercise book and composing some imaginary tale.

It wasn't, no doubt owing to my failure, the field of the screenplay that occupied my attention. I turned to fiction. Between the ages of thirteen and sixteen – when I was seduced again from prose by the alluring siren of poetry, after hearing our coppery-voiced English master, Jerry Claypole, reading Masefield's *Reynard the Fox* aloud – I completed no less than half a dozen full-length novels, ranging in theme from detective stories to science fiction.

All of these are awful. They show an amazing lack of talent – amazing, at any rate, to one who has subsequently tried to scrape his living from just this field, the popular novel.

Perhaps, after all, I still meant to be a runner. I was doing no more than mark time before I could bend again to the chalk line, go up on my toes, and sprint for a distant tape, arms in and head back, with nothing out in front except air and grass.

It may, after all, be a widespread fantasy. I was not alone, I suspect, in feeling a lump come to my throat when the Scottish sprinter went out ahead to win the Olympic 400 metres in *Chariots of Fire*. No literary success could ever be as satisfying as that.

18

It was quite early in my teens that I mastered the art of masturbation. I know that over a year was exhausted in fruitless experiment, yanking an inert member to and fro, while attempting to conjure up images of Betty Grable's legs.

What finally achieved the desired, albeit unexpected result, was less, I think, the result of improved technique, than of a suitable visual aid. I still recall vividly, though I no longer possess the magazine, the inspiring cover of *The Man* which ultimately provoked my first emission of semen.

The experience was not, in fact, very pleasurable. It was frightening. Nobody had told me that there would be a sudden uncontrollable urgency, like an onset of diarrhoea, and what squirmed unexpectedly into my palm, like the rush of glue from a recalcitrant tube, seemed meagre, disgusting and pallid.

I'd been anticipating something much whiter and thicker, like Maclean's toothpaste, and for some months I seriously believed I had something wrong with me, and was producing a sperm tainted with an alien swirl, like the colouring in a tin of paint when it separates from the oil.

Attempts to stir my own tin of paint only tended to produce further disappointing mixtures, like egg yolk broken into white in a pan, as when I would stand and finger myself in the lavatory, while anxious to pass water. On these occasions, a strange prickling surge would further convince me that I had some debilitating illness.

It may be that remorse was already mingling with desire in the traditional Puritan brew. Indeed, the two together continue, for many people, to supply a heady cocktail.

In my own case, that first, initiatory emission may have been helped by a sense of pressure, not only of finger on foreskin, but of time and risk of exposure. I was examining the magazine in the comparative privacy of my bedroom, but there was no lock on the door, and my mother, if she had wanted me for anything, would have walked in without knocking.

In adult retrospect it seems astonishing to suppose that an attractive middle-aged woman would have been shocked at the sight of her adolescent son crouched over a folded colour picture of a girl in a bathing suit, with an engorged penis in his trembling hand. She would far more likely have been oddly excited, or obscurely moved, or even, perhaps, a little saddened.

What she would have done about these emotions is another matter. She would probably have done nothing, pretending not to notice what was going on. Indeed, I do recall her adopting this strategy on one or two later, slightly more ambiguous occasions.

Nevertheless, embarrassment, and a furtive anxiety not to be caught, seem to have continued as the contributory elements to a good outcome, at least so long as the joys of sex were experienced alone. And this was for several years.

At the age of fourteen I was in love with Evelyn Keyes. I had first seen her kneeling on a beach, in the central pages of *The Bulletin*, posing for a publicity pin-up for her forthcoming role in *The Jolson Story*.

Later, I secretly bought a film magazine, with a pink-sepia photograph of her torso on the cover. I kept this tucked away under piles of *Hotspur*s in my bedroom box, and would surreptitiously take it out, and stare in gooey tenderness into the star's huge eyes, before I lay down to sleep.

In due course I discovered, in one of Teddy Stokes's *Men Only*s, an elegant photograph of Jesse Matthews, head only, which also stressed her enormous, long-lashed eyes. This I furtively ripped out, stole, and hid inside the magazine with Evelyn Keyes.

Between the two of them, I now enjoyed the silent services of a beautiful wife and a beautiful mistress. Both seemed to me exquisitely pretty, and I could no more choose between them than between my left hand and my right.

The eyes seem to have been the thing. Great, lustrous,

all-consuming, humorous-tender, fascinating eyes. The purer image, in retrospect, seems to have been the isolated head of Jesse Matthews, hair drawn up into a high bun on top of her head, leaving the neck and the ears bare and vulnerable. Indeed, perhaps there was an unconscious reminiscence here of my mother's head as I bent to wash her back in the bath.

Evelyn Keyes, too, was revealed in exactly the same way, but with the additional, disturbing element of a sensuously full bust, arched under a sculpted cantilever of brassière, and lightly shrouded under a gauze blouse.

Despite this openly seductive torso, however, and the arm set provokingly on a narrow waist, I never in my teens found this image other than lyrically uplifting. Neither Evelyn Keyes, nor Jesse Matthews, was ever the object of masturbation fantasy. It was enough to look at their faces, and to dream.

Clearly, I was effectively bifurcated by a schizophrenia of love and lust. I had been brought up to think of a girl as someone you fell in love with, staring adoringly into her eyes, and perhaps, at some supreme moment, holding her hand and even kissing her on the lips.

My animal nature, almost by accident, had stumbled upon the quite separate allure, as it then seemed, of a woman's body below the neck, a landscape of breasted mountain and ridge of thigh, cloven by the long mysterious belly valley that ran to some hinted-at, though still never envisaged, cavern of desire.

Contemplating images of mature women, thus richly endowed with a contrasting profile of peaks and troughs, and quite unlike the boyish androgynes I would fall in love with, seemed to lead fairly inevitably to a quickening shiver of lustfulness which demanded the attention of hand rather than eye.

I had no way to reconcile these emotional and physical urges. I remember the prurient excitement with which I read the opening pages of John O'Hara's *Appointment in Samaria*, where a small boy runs under a woman's long dress, and she is described as closing her legs, but not before his little fingers have got where they wanted to.

This was the same year, and could easily have been the

same day, that I wept with a mingled sense of loss and joy when a dark-haired beauty from the Girl's High School smiled at me across a crowded room.

They say that the British Army advanced five miles in the Falaise Gap on the day that Jane finally took her knickers off in the *Daily Mirror*. In my own body, such a transference of sexual energy into action could find no athletic outlet.

It may be that my role as an invalid with a bad heart accentuated the usual adolescent reluctance to have anything to do with girls. At any rate, I didn't. I turned instead, as others have done, to a sublimated affection for a number of junior boys.

One of these, whose name was Timperley, had an exalting alto voice, and I would listen to him singing in the school choir with a sense of approaching an angel in heaven. One smiles, in retrospect, at such an abstract and undemanding satisfaction, but it was undeniably a powerful source of delight at the time.

The only boy whom I conceive myself to have been in love with, however, was Copeland. I don't now remember his Christian name and, of course, I would never have addressed him by this. We were a surname school, Victorian, dour and male.

Copeland was then a slender, dark-skinned, fine-featured boy with sparkling eyes, who must have been about three years younger than I was. He would now be a man in advancing middle age, no doubt with a family and a responsible job. The idea is hard to accept.

So far as I can satisfy myself, and it may be on this matter that memory is a hostile witness, I never experienced anything akin to an erection, either in contemplation of, or in contact with, this boy.

I do know that I felt a great sweetness in any physical proximity, such as playing billiards, or sitting together watching a film. I remember a dream, too, in which I was carrying Copeland in my arms out of a burning building.

Whether or not he responded to my sense of closeness I no longer know. It was never voiced, for sure. We certainly seem to have spent some time together, and some of it in teasing and gentle horseplay. The mind boggles at what I may have forgotten. But forgotten I certainly have.

The most dramatic, and concluding, episode of our relationship, if it might be called any such committed thing, was the making of a school film. This film, a project of the Cinema Club which had first interested me in writing, was to involve a holiday on location, near to where the school Scout troop, of which Copeland was a prominent member, was holding its summer camp.

There was a vacancy for a scriptwriter on the film and I applied for, and got, this job. The director was Michael Dawson, an outlaw and an aesthete, whose anarchic objections to singing *God Save the King* had been siphoned into other channels. The assistant director was John Bingham.

The central character in the film was a dead dog. In those days of *Bicycle Thieves* and Italian verismo, no papier mâché or imaginary animal would have been acceptable. This meant that some person or persons had to obtain, transport and, subsequently, preserve one actual member of the canine species, defunct.

This job fell, for some reason, to John Bingham and myself. The dog was bought, in the sultriest of August weather, from a Sheffield vet and, wrapped in a travelling bag, borne on the luggage rack of a crowded train down to Ross-on-Wye.

From there it was taken, I think by bus, to the camp site near to Goodrich, where the film was to be shot. Every night the corpse would be buried, and every morning, with increasing misgivings, exhumed.

The plot of the film involved a Scout, who suffered a nervous breakdown after seeing a favourite dog run over by a train. The boy's eventual fate now escapes me, but he climbed, at one point, to the summit of a local mountain, Symonds Yat, from which, like all of us in due course, he enjoyed a good view of Wales.

The shooting, like the shooting of so many films, was

fraught with emotion, intrigue, and delay. Dawson, who was an imaginative director, was a poor organiser. John Bingham, who was quite a good organiser, was excessively slow and argumentative. I was interested only in my health, my yellow waistcoat, and Copeland.

One of the problems of my health was that my mother had refused to allow me to sleep under canvas, as the other members of the crew were doing, and so I retired, each evening, in solitary splendour, to a rented bedroom in a nearby cottage.

From there I would emerge, refreshed and frustrated, to drink huge measures of draught cider, fortified, as they used to say, with steaks, and to hear of nightly forays, the subject of recrimination and quarrel, to the well-stocked cellars of Goodrich Castle, an early Victorian pile sited across the valley from the ruins of a genuine fifteenth-century castle, and later bought and removed stone by stone to Texas.

The film was never finished. The rushes, or the stock, or whatever it was all called, returned to Sheffield with Dawson, and was never edited. The crew, too, returned home, and the camp broke up, and the dog remained buried, and my relationship with Copeland came to an end.

There had been nothing final, simply a boredom, a lack of closeness, and a pressure of alternative interests. Perhaps, after all, this is how so many passions die away, less with a bang than a whimper.

My first experience of sex with a woman occurred when I was eighteen. It was by no means edifying. Tales of prowess with girls were commonplace at school, and the pressure to make some beginning oneself was a strong one.

In my own case, I'm sure that I could never have managed without help from friends. In the event, these friends turned out to be Ian Martin, now a strapping young Adonis with marcelled blond hair, and a rather lascivious, girlish boy with large teeth and a perpetual grin, called Peter Green.

Between them they had somehow secured the services of a considerably older, clearly experienced woman who now comes back as aged about twenty-four, and who wore a mauve two-piece suit. I was invited by Ian Martin and Peter Green to go for a walk with them and this girl.

It was made quite clear that it was to be a walk with a purpose. I agreed. On what I recall as a bright and warm afternoon, we set out, no doubt after a now forgotten bus ride, across one of Sheffield's many surrounding hills.

In due course there was a pause to enjoy the view, and we all sat down on the grass. There must have been some screening hummock, or hollow, since I recall we three boys taking it in turns to retire with the lady in the mauve two-piece to somewhere that felt more private.

This may be beginning to sound like a kind of gang-bang, or perhaps an encounter with a prostitute. No doubt the hackles of any feminist, male or female, who may happen to be reading, have already risen. However, the event was neither of these things. To begin with, I don't believe that the woman was paid. In the second place, I recall that she was the instigator, and indeed the engineer, of whatever was done. Whatever satisfaction was obtained, in the hasty, semi-public, and fumbled intromissions of our triune excitement, I doubt if her sense of guilt, outrage and obscure shame was in the same class as our own.

On the contrary, I see her now as distinctively nympho-maniac, a liker of boys, and almost motherly in her willing-ness to allow us to try out our new-found masculinity. We were virgins, hardly raped for sure, but certainly woman-handled.

So that what returns is less the sense of rumpled knickers, and splayed, freckled flesh, than squatting before the event on the edge of the hummock, nervously picking tufts of grass, and staring down at the valley, like a patient in a dentist's waiting-room, not exactly sure how painful the filling will be.

Perhaps I was remembering the legends of the Bradford mill-girls, who were supposed to lie in wait for unsuspecting men, strip them, and force their limp penises into jam-jars filled with wasps. They would then tease and stimulate the men, so it was said, until the wasps, first attracted by the smell and stickiness of the aroused and extended erections, and then annoyed by their jerky twitching, would insert their belligerent stings, injecting poison into what the mill-girls believed already contained poison.

Swallow that, you'll swallow anything, I now believe. But it was a potent myth at the time, as the *vagina dentata* had been before. It was less a honey-pot that I anticipated than a dangerous hive.

19

The years after my illness have a tendency to telescope. They were all informed by the same problems, the same aura. However, this private consistency was matched by a unity of theme in the public world of the wireless and the newspapers.

The war had ended, yes. But the war had never ended. Rationing was as bad as ever. I remember that the weekly butter allowance was still only two ounces when I went up to Oxford as late as 1951.

Despite the arrival of the New Look, with the drop in hem-lines and the disappearance of women's calves under tight sheaths with gussets, the materials of which clothes were made were all Utility. Every book still bore a preliminary statement that it was printed in accordance with wartime economy standards.

Military personnel, and military vehicles, were everywhere. Demobbing progressed at a snail's pace. No sooner had the Germans been defeated, and then the Japanese, than the Russians emerged as the enemy, and the Cold War succeeded the hot one.

It was hard to see much change. Even the much-vaunted defeat of the Conservative Government, and the banishment to the wilderness of Winston Churchill, our great war leader, seemed to produce little alteration in the familiar faces in the magazines. Clement Attlee had been deputy Prime Minister, now he was Prime Minister. It looked very much, to a schoolboy used to the promotion of prefects, as if it had simply become his turn.

The independence of India, and the nationalisation of the railways and the mines, were undoubtedly momentous events, but they were announced with all the fanfaronade of military victories, and their impact on my own everyday life was minimal.

The only Indians I ever saw were soldiers of the Queen. The trains were still full of soldiers, and our fires were still fuelled with coal. All in all, it seemed that the war was continuing to tick over, as it had done since 1941, with a remote, threatening, but not immediate importance.

It simply formed the strategic backcloth for the hand-to-hand fighting in the bullring of school.

On one trip to Scotland I was taken by my mother to see some cousins of hers who all lived together in an old house at Glassford. There were three of them at this time, a man and two women, all over seventy. None had ever married.

At one time, I believe they had been five, but I never discovered, or asked about, the fate of the other two. You might have supposed they would have died, and that would have been all that there was to it, except that there was a curious aura over Glassford which seemed to preserve everything as if in amber, and halt time in its tracks.

Glassford was notorious for its absence of change, and for a will towards an absence of change. My Aunt Margaret would mutter endlessly about the evils of harbouring dirt, and cluttering the house up with useless lumber, and not keeping in touch with the modern world.

Everything there was preserved. Nothing, with the exception of decaying food matter, was ever thrown away. For thirty years, every single newspaper that had come into the house had been read, folded, and then piled up against a wall. Every empty tin of tobacco smoked by the man of the house was retained and slid into place on top of one of the teetering cylinders in the study. Every worn-out blouse or petticoat was aired and stored in mothballs in its appropriate drawer.

So omnipresent were the gathered files of disposable things – bus tickets under elastic bands, bills for meat and groceries tied up in little bows of string, wrappings of former Christmas presents laid away in boxes – that I have no recollection at all of the appearance or characteristics, other than their will to collect and retain, of any of the three old people.

They were entirely unpacked and externalised into the physical relics of their everyday experiences, a sort of Kurt Schwitters collage of trivia, lovingly extracted from the dustbin and the waste-paper basket and mounted on the tiny canvas of their shared cottage.

I found these materialised lives fascinating, crowding in at me from every corner and alcove – a tumbling, dusty, ancient, enduring monument to the gritty paraphernalia of day-by-day living. This was a touchable museum of a world stretching back before I was born, a door into the past through which, like Alice, I could step into febrile fantasy solid still with fact.

So far as I know, I was taken only once to Glassford, but its influence was substantial. It made me realise, as I had never done before, how resonant with feeling mere things could be. It made me treasure my old toys and comics. It made me decide, too, that, when I inherited them, I would also treasure whatever things had belonged to my father.

Alas, the Glassford objects were treasured no more after the death of the last of the sisters.

My Aunt Margaret, inheriting the property with ill-concealed satisfaction, prepared a monstrous bonfire, searing through an eon of private and unrecapturable history in a single blaze of flame. What might have escaped the fire was knocked down at auction, and the lives of the Glassford cousins were finally reduced, like most other people's, to a bundle of memories.

My own cousins had now begun to separate away, and marry, and rear their own families. I was much the youngest on my mother's side, although I had younger – two younger – on my father's. Inevitably, it is the older cousins who return most vividly to mind. Neither Greta nor Finlay is other than a shadowy child in my recollection.

Their brother Andrew, however, is a looming presence. He was very close to my father, as my father seems to have been to him, and I think of Andrew as the nearest thing to the brother I never had. We see each other rarely now, but the meetings are fraught with emotion.

When I was younger, Andrew seemed to be a much bigger boy, harsh and clear in his Scottishness, and always operating as a sort of conscience, or code hero, in keeping me up to an audible mark of Caledonian correctness, preventing any backsliding into southern namby-pambiness.

Now that I am taller than he is, though far less broad and strong, he still presents himself to my eye as a dourly Calvinist figure, albeit one oddly transmogrified into a spirit of eccentric irony, offering me shortbread in tartan boxes, and conveying advice from the north in elliptic sentences.

I know that Andrew has never had money to squander, but he emerges as a figure of burning pride, able to travel abroad, and buy meals, and live in expensive hotels. Both of my wives have admired him, a rare tribute, and, when I think of him, I feel a mixture of responsibility and affection, as if my father were stepping through my own bones.

None of my other cousins, economically so much more successful, arouses quite such deep feelings. One or two, such as my Uncle David's daughter Jean, and the trio of Dundee girls, have been too long out of touch to remain more than glimpses through a curtained window, the 1940s world of crocodile handbags and arranged stocking seams in which I see them preserved as lipsticked adolescents.

When I close my eyes, my Cousin Willie is the re-incarnation of my Uncle Hugh, a voice as rich as the variations of granite in which his father used to build, but when I open them again, time has drifted and he stands there as a dark-haired boy in a kilt, in the corner of the photograph at my mother and father's wedding.

The adult Willie of the 1940s, whom family legend would imagine as a Byronic figure, spoiled and adventurous, peeks out from behind the friendly man who offers me a good cigar, plucked like a skean-dhu from the top of his thermal sock, and who speaks of never stopping, on his drives to London, because if you do you have to pass all the other cars again.

One mark of the difference between my mother's and my father's families is that my Cousin Willie inherited and owned the brickworks next to May Street where my Cousin Andrew worked as a labourer. But I doubt that either of them has ever met.

In the later 1940s, as I grew to school-leaving age, these cousins were all lodged in their own lives, married or unmarried, rich or poor, close or remote. They existed then as the lower echelon of a family structure more immediately familiar to me as the upper strata of aunt and uncle. Now that the years have taken their toll, the circle has closed, and this outer resonance of blood's echoes, pulsing with the remaining beat of all that the twinned family heart set moving, rings in my ears, and matters more, and is all I have.

I sometimes feel that I walk in a killing ground, and the floor has been cleared of the living all around me, leaving only my eleven cousins, waving from their own lives, across a scorched abyss.

Scotland welded me closer to my mother. England eased me apart. Our interests, as I grew older, were more obviously different than they had seemed when I was a child. I wasn't, for example, at all musical, and was unable to follow in her fingerprints as a player of the piano.

This may have given her more cause for grief than I saw at the time. I wasn't even much interested in singing, or songs. Nor was I practical enough to share her interest in gardening, or in cooking.

I used to make pancake men, when very small, and I would enjoy dropping the raisins for their eyes into the creamy mixture of their bodies as it started to grow brown on the griddle; but this play-cooking never developed into anything more mature.

When I look into my mother's recipe book, and remember on my tongue, or my mind's tongue, the savour of almost-forgotten dishes, cakes and puddings and confectionery, I realise that I hold in my hand, were I more skilful, the means to re-enact some of the most tasty and pleasurable products of her talents.

However, the urge to roll dough, and to ice cakes, and to grease tins for bonfire toffee, and to mix a chocolate sauce to go over Rice Krispies, has never borne much fruit, or much pastry either, for that matter. I can no more match my mother in boiling potatoes rolled in oatmeal than I can equal my father in cleaning a sparking plug.

The practical skills have passed me by. When I was in my

teens this would occasionally upset my mother, but only, I think, if it seemed to provide evidence for what she would regard as laziness. Active as she always was herself, she could never bear hands to be idle.

Indeed, one of the few occasions on which I remember her losing her temper was when I was dilatory in lending a helping hand with the moving of some rubbish in the garden. For a few seconds she shook, literally, with rage. I was aware of how physically strong she seemed, unexpectedly so.

But she never hit me, or used any other form of force, or much coercion either. I suspect that she felt so frightened by my illness, and so grateful that I survived, that she relieved me of any strenuous burden, lest it affect my heart.

I developed, therefore, invalid as I became, into a creature of the mind rather than the body. I began to read, as I had always done, for pleasure, but now also to lay bare the springs of power, to broaden my experience, and to fuel my skills.

Poetry, in particular, became the gateway to a new career, the glamorising of the banal. I discovered a soulmate in the exotic persona of James Elroy Flecker, whose premature death from consumption at the age of thirty-two seemed to prefigure, in suitably far-off resonance, my own potential demise from an incurable disease.

I liked the rhythm of Flecker's verse, and its gaudy diction. I still do, and I probably know more of him by heart than any other poet. Our lodger, Miss Green, would no doubt be surprised by this. She had the effrontery to tell me once that enjoying Flecker was the mark of an immature mind, a stage that one simply went through.

But then those were the 1940s, when immortal figures such as Henry Treece were in vogue.

20

The major arena of my education became the Public Library, a white stone building of no architectural merit across the road from the Town Hall. A flicker of grim romance was attached to the lobby, through which one entered the library, by the fact that a suicide had once hurled himself down on to the tiles from the Art Gallery balcony, three floors above.

In general, though, the library was a prosaic and a silencing place. The books, on open shelves, provided me with access to Blake and Cecil Day Lewis, and later to Carl Sandburg and Robert Lowell. I read voraciously.

I think the cliché is accurate. I was hungry for poetry, once I got into it, and the addiction has remained. Flecker beckoned me from his Consular Service blazer, white and crumpled, with a swastika on the pocket, more sinister there, reversed though it was, than the golden ones on the spines of *The Jungle Book* and *Puck of Pook's Hill*.

Auden caught my attention with his shielded cigarette, a smoker like my father. Keith Douglas was almost the same age as myself, a young blood in a knotted scarf, serious against his tank after the battle of Alamein.

It was often less the poems, in fact, than the poets, the identifiable transmitting agencies of the magic, yet as ordinary themselves as ticket-collectors and seamen, who captured my imagination. I began to dream myself one of them, black hair – which I don't have – sleaked down like Louis MacNeice's.

At the top of the building, the Art Gallery began to furnish my imagination with painterly visions as the library at the bottom supplied it with verbal dreams. The two would sometimes coincide.

The first exhibition I saw was a retrospective for Paul Nash – to my militaristic eye less of a surrealist than a war artist, with his foot in the 1916 trenches on the Somme and his hand on the joystick of the Lancasters above the clouds on their way to Frankfurt.

I was impressed by the Nash diaries, and would soon be reading Dali and Le Corbusier, drunk on the mixture of words and pictures which has remained, over many years, the most exhilarating for me of the pleasures books can offer.

I read widely, enjoying both Herrick and Edgar Lee Masters. More and more books would ride home in my small, battered suitcase, the mistresses for an evening's intellectual debauchery. But fewer and fewer of them would be shared with my mother.

Perhaps it was becoming necessary to establish an independent eyrie of the spirit, somewhere that would be inaccessible − like the private lockable room I never had − to even the most exacting and reasonable demands of love.

I hate to think this. But the growth seems clear. I wanted my own world, one shared, if at all, only by those of my own age. For a year or two I developed into someone very ordinary, just like any other adolescent, rebellious and lonely.

It didn't last. The sunk keels of the great battleships of trauma were too deep in the salt bottom of my bloodstream for that. My mother was more important than any books were ever going to be.

Very soon, I would know just how important.

Curiously enough, in view of my interest in books, I never realised in her lifetime that my mother owned a copy of Palgrave's *Golden Treasury*. It may not, of course, have impressed my un-Victorian mind in those days that she did. Still, it has occurred to me in retrospect that it would at least have opened up some channel of communication about poetry.

I obviously didn't want one. I was already too far out in the great sea of emotion on my own, and not waving, as it were, but drowning. The presence of another craft in hailing distance, or even in telescope sight, would have seemed an interference.

My mother's Palgrave is a little red volume, with incised pillars, and gold lettering. Only one poem has been marked by her, and that is ringed with a blue crayon, 'The Lament for Flodden'.

I didn't know the poem, until I read it there, and then I did know why my mother had been so touched by it, and had ringed it in blue, royal blue, as I think of it, like the blood of a king.

The battle of Flodden Field was a great defeat for King James, and the poem is an elegy for his men who fell, fighting the English. 'The flowers of the forest, who fought aye the foremost, the pride of our Scotland, lie cauld in the clay.'

There may be better lines about a soldier dying, and my mother may have known some of them, but these verses must have summed up for her what my father was: both a creature of transitory beauty who had been cut down in his prime, like a flower, and a human being and a Scotsman who was no longer alive in the warm sun, but underground in the earth, at Crookes, where we still went to be with him, as near as we could.

I wish we might have shared the poem, while there was still time. But we shared my father, and that, after all, is what matters.

Towards the end of my teens there was an acceleration of intellectual interests. I began to take part, for example, in school plays. The Dramatic Society was under the control, as was the school magazine, which printed some of my early poems, of the senior Latin master, E. F. Watling, a tall gaunt man, like a diving-board set up on end.

At this time, the later 1940s, he was achieving some fame in the wake of E. V. Rieu – author of our prose Homer and butcher of Butcher and Lang – as the Penguin translator of Sophocles. His lean, wiry versions deserved their wide circulation. They provided some antidote, rightly thought necessary in an austerity decade, to the John Drinkwater treatment meted out by Gilbert Murray.

Old Watling – we always called masters old, whatever their age, though, in fact, old Watling was probably not much beyond his late forties – was an effective and an enterprising director, who kept an eye on what was new. He was unsuccessful, through no fault of his own, in getting permission from Christopher Fry for a school production of *Moses*, in which I had been cast in the title role.

This might have coloured my responses to someone then seen as the white hope of British drama, but it didn't. I saw and adored *A Phoenix Too Frequent* in a closet production at the International Centre, and for a few weeks my own verses were clustered with gaudy, inept images, and lax rhythms.

I did perform in *The Playboy of the Western World*, where the scene-stealing role of Old Mahon formed the climax of my career, a club-wielding, older-than-my-age cameo which allowed some synthesis of aggression with whiskery make-up, two staples of my style. I suppose that it was consoling, too, to play the role of a father who returns from the dead.

In an earlier production of Maxwell Anderson's *Winterset*, I had lain under a table through the big scene in the role of the hobo, a tongue-tied derelict whose main line, several times repeated, is 'I got a piece of bread.' I greatly admired the romantic realism of *Winterset*, with its rhetoric of free verse lines drawing on the sweep of Shakespeare, and I can still mouth some of Mio's Hamlet-like verses on the death of his father in the electric chair.

> *That night, the guards*
> *Walking in flood-lights brighter than high noon*
> *Led him between them, with his trousers slit*
> *And a shaven head for the cathodes.*

This kind of American protest-writing strikes me now as much better than the Festival of Britain frothiness of Christopher Fry. It may be, however, that I am still under the spell of the James Cagney myth. *Angels with Dirty Faces* echoes powerfully in the background of *Winterset*, and the gangster Trock Estrella, as he dies of consumption, is cast in the mould of Macbeth. How could I fail to be impressed as this bleak, surrogate hero apostrophised New York?

> *You roost of punks and gulls!*
> *Get down one big ham fat against another.*
> *Sleep, dream and rot!*

Strong stuff to my adolescent ear, not least in a situation where an occasional punch-line could be extracted and used for mockery of one's friends, John Bingham as Ham providing an apt target for the second line quoted above.

Bingham, in fact, though less of a mummer as time went on, had played opposite me the previous year in a production of R. C. Sherriff's *Journey's End*, where I was cast as the sergeant-major who carries the wounded Raleigh down into the dug-out on his back.

We had only a moderately heavy Raleigh, but he was far too much for me, and so the additional role of a soldier, non-speaking, was created for John Bingham as the production's understudy. I recall that we still had trouble between the two of us, lugging the living weight through a flimsy backcloth. It was a good deal more awkward than a dead dog.

The sergeant, of course, is usually a burly, substantial actor, and the clothes hired for him in our production were vastly too large. They inaugurated, no doubt, both my interest in military gear, and my sense that it would always be, symbolically and sometimes literally, the wrong size for me.

A set of cartoons remains in my filing cabinet, sent to me by their artist, the school physics master, whom we always knew as Trotsky, because of his neat, small beard. He drew these cartoons in careful crayon in 1950, and sent them to me nearly thirty years later, as the only member of the cast he was able to get in touch with, wanting his drawing, and the memory of the production, to survive his approaching death.

I was touched by this concern. The cartoons will indeed survive, fossilised on khaki paper, a crayon memorial of a play, a greasepaint equivalent for the landscape of cordite and mud, wire and gas, where my two uncles died in 1918.

School plays were an officially condoned interest. Several of my other preoccupations were not. From our early teens John Bingham and I had collaborated in a number of more or less illegitimate business ventures, most more imaginative than money-making, though the obtaining of extra cash was normally their motive.

I seem to have possessed a Lowland Scotsman's shrewd eye for a financial opportunity. I once sold John Bingham the Law of Multiple Proportions for sixpence in a mathematics exam. Unfortunately, we were caught, and made to write out a hundred times, the notorious Cribber's Hymn.

> *Yield not to temptation*
> *For Yielding is sin.*
> *Each victory helps us*
> *Another to win.*

Echoes of the Western Desert and the Italian Campaign resound from those last two lines. I like to think that I learned a lesson against risking too quick a buck from this experience.

I passed on to the slower processes of usury, and would lend a rather feckless boy with the military-sounding name of Gordon sums ranging from one to five pounds a time, at outrageous rates of interest. I'm not quite sure why he needed the money – for gambling, I think – but he always agreed to my demands, and he accepted philosophically my insistence on increases if he failed to pay on time. He later entered the army, and for all I know may still be there.

One of my earlier ventures with John Bingham was a Photography Service. We were prepared to take portrait studies, either of individuals or groups, and to supply contact prints either singly or in quantity.

I still have some of our prints. The rather shy, hunched figure of Brian Jessup, later a crack writer of Latin verses, peers out from a miasma of cloudy residue around his shoulders. Jack Hallows, who had to be taken to four churches before his father could find a priest who would christen him Jack, lolls back on a mass of boys in a group, grinning widely.

I remember the dim rituals of developing and printing, shrouding our kitchen windows as though for a return of the black-out, and bending like a wizard over bowls of hypo where the grey images would slowly creep to view from a glossy contact paper.

Life took place in a rosy glow at those times, but the

Photography Service failed to last. The fertile, restless mind of John Bingham was already elsewhere, elaborating ever more subtle forms of Buccaneer, or his own invention, a game known as Conquistadore, in which Cortés and his men were beset by Indians in their trek through virgin jungle.

We shared other ventures, not always in full collaboration, and in time there would be an advertisement in the *Sheffield Star* for The MacBeth Baby Sitting Bureau, an ill-starred operation which took the supposed proprietor's name in vain.

However, by far the most enduring, and most frowned upon, of our many shared endeavours was the League For Democratic Action, very shortly to be more concisely known as the Sheffield Anti-Communist League.

21

John Bingham was a political thinker far more original and advanced than I. His reading embraced the anarcho-syndicalists and the Italian economist Pareto, and he was aware of minor National Socialist poets such as the prematurely dying Dietrich Eckhart.

My own political vice was for a kind of militant patriotism, largely based on a thin reading of Ruskin's *The Crown of Wild Olive*, where he speaks of every right-thinking man as preferring, if allowed the choice, to be sculpted with a broad sword rather than a cricket bat.

I had stood, unsuccessfully, in a school election as a Liberal, and was later involved in some dreary committee work for a local constituency association, and the occasional uninspiring distribution of leaflets. This was the age of the Liberal decline rather than its revival, and there was small glamour for a thirsty activist.

In 1950 a British warship, the *Amethyst*, was shelled by the Red Chinese while sailing peacefully down the Yangtze River. This widely reported scandal, and the failure of the Labour Government to initiate satisfactory reprisals, impelled John Bingham to campaign among us in support of a protest march to be routed through the commercial heart of Sheffield, chanting slogans and carrying flags.

I fell in with this plan. The notion of a totally anarchic, and possibly illegal, parade of paramilitary strength through a public place, and on a Saturday afternoon, was quite irresistible. The cause was of secondary importance.

Unfortunately, John Bingham was struck down – as if God Himself had gone Red – by a sudden attack of infantile paralysis over the very days of the final planning. I went to see him in hospital, and he gave me his instructions from a bed of pain, but the organisation of the event fell squarely upon me.

It was the beginning of a year of power. I was able to

sustain the interest of about eighteen or twenty sixth-formers, who in due course did march, led by a boy called Findlay, later to be the editor of the local newspaper and the exposer of police brutality in the use of a rhinoceros-hide whip. He marched in front, waving a large Union Jack.

I walked alongside like a Roman centurion, dressing the line, exhorting the faint-hearted and the lazy, and initiating the periodic shouts of 'What About The *Amethyst*?' and 'Outlaw the Reds', which punctuated our progress.

This march, though unofficial, was allowed to continue for some distance by the police, and it was later reported in full in the *Sheffield Telegraph*, complete with a photograph.

The event was noted both by the left and the right, and in due course, upon John Bingham returning from hospital – tough as before, though with a slight limp ominous enough to remind us of the fate of Franklyn D. Roosevelt whose polio had forced him to fight his elections from a wheelchair – we had membership cards printed, and were no longer a march, but a movement.

The Anti-Communist League was often misunderstood. I was once stopped in Barker's Pool by our very serious-faced minister from St Andrew's, who said that he was very disappointed to hear rumours that I had become a Communist.

Others were equally disapproving. The committee of a local Conservative Association, when approached for support, advised us that the main enemy was the Labour Party, and that we would be better employed raising our flag against them.

Our main ally was the Economic League, a vaguely right-wing body funded, I suppose, by capitalist neurosis and existing to combat economic dissent fomented, as they conceived or observed it, by the British Communist Party. They would arrange outings to heckle Arthur Horner, the left-wing leader of the Miners' Union, and were once keen to see if we could be got tickets for the World Peace Congress in Sheffield City Hall, where the Red Dean of Westminster was to fulminate against the Marxlessness of the established Church.

I recall solemn meetings with Commander Long, an extremely handsome, rather aristocratic figure of thirty-eight, who was rumoured to have been the model for Ian Fleming's James Bond. His dark suits and his long cigarette holder created an air of elegance and clubland heroism which gave a flattering tinge of John Buchanism to our efforts.

Nevertheless, these efforts were largely fruitless, mundane or bizarre. There was a certain amount of boring leaflet-dispensing, and some soap-box oratory, but the more appealing ventures, at least to me, included a hazardous expedition one dark night to paint a slogan in flashing whitewash along the school wall, and some weeks spent rehearsing and recording two imaginary radio newsreels, purporting to dramatise the real truth about the Communist seizure of power in Czechoslovakia in 1948, and the conditions prevalent in East European prisons.

I played a weak Liberal Prime Minister on one of these gramophone recordings, calling in a woefully lisping voice, which only this recording told me that I possessed, for calm and order in the face of disruption. Michael Dawson, more raspingly, provided the sharp voice of a revolutionary agitator.

The idea was that the recordings would be played in youth clubs, and initiate political discussion, but I don't recall that there was ever much demand for them. Most youth clubs, like the Methodist one I attended myself to play table tennis, were more interested in Jean Cocteau films, or in dancing, than in pursuing the arguments of their sixth-form International Discussion Groups.

Our own International Discussion Group once had a visit from Geoffrey Hamm, a frail ghost of a man, whose blue eyes were always watchful, as if for a brick thrown, or perhaps only in bemused retrospect of the 1936 Olympia rally and the ball-bearings rolling under the hooves of the police horses.

Mosley had been invited, but it was Hamm we got, an organiser and an acolyte. He was received with polite aggression, and questioned closely. The balance was kept by the invitation of an eminent Marxist historian.

The streets beckoned, though, and it was more fun to ride on the back of a motor bike to a draughty hall where someone had to be heckled than to lounge around a littered table in the school library and put one's civil questions with the word 'sir' at the end.

Empty rant and blind action, only half-jokingly thus dismissed, were the modes of our political endeavour. They governed our dreams and our practice. Alas, in the light of this dangerous philosophy it was a pity that I held to my view that there was nothing one could not do in one's best suit.

I returned home once with a long tear in the knee of my trousers, placating my distressed mother with the excuse that I had fallen off a tram. In fact, this clothing wound had been received in a tactical withdrawal from a coffee bar, where three of us had been beleaguered, watching the leader of a numerically superior force of Young Communists, Godfrey Jones, taking off his tie in preparation for an assault.

Our retreat had been covered, mercifully, by the arrival of that traditional security symbol, a British policeman. But the hint of violence was still there, symbolic in cloth, and later filled with stitches like the scar in my brow.

Violence receded, but it came again, and from an unexpected quarter. One night a group of us were walking past a police station from John Bingham's house at Meadowhead, singing a drunken song at the tops of our voices, when two overzealous constables came out and laid into us with their fists.

Peter Sinclair, now a mathematics don at Oxford, came off worst. I, lucky as always, got away scot-free.

My main lieutenant in the Anti-Communist League was a boy called Bertie Round, slightly younger than I, moon-faced and a crack swimmer. He had a project to be the youngest man ever to swim the Channel, and he did, in fact, swim the length of Lake Windermere in preparation for this, but for some now forgotten reason, lack of financial backing perhaps, the bid for the record never took place.

Bertie was a noted rake as well as a famed swimmer. Perhaps the skilful manipulation of the limbs is essential for both vocations. At any rate, he could recount a list of some thirty-eight mistresses before he was seventeen, and either a fine imagination or a sound memory had included surprisingly authentic details.

Our first encounter was in the world of ice-cream. A slightly older boy, Norman Adsetts, had a father who was then the largest ice-cream manufacturer − after Wall's and Lyons − in the north of England, and he had the shrewd notion of inviting his son to employ boys from King Edward's to sell wafers at football and cricket matches at Bramall Lane, the home ground of Sheffield United.

Every Saturday afternoon, a band of embryo salesmen would ride by van to the ground, assume the white coat and the shoulder-slung tray of the professional vendor, and launch themselves, raucous-voiced, into the midst of the crowd on Spion Kop.

The salary, at first a fixed one, was three half-crowns − or half-dollars as they were still known in those sterling-strong years − and this money was paid out at the end of the day in clinking silver. I went proudly home to my mother with a trio of stamped coins like small medals, a solid reward for virtue.

At first, Norman Adsetts himself was in charge of the sales force, but, in due course, he left school for the army, and a successor had to be found. The responsibility, and also a small extra kickback, fell to me. I marshalled my men as before, and sales maintained their level.

Bertie Round, however, was the star of the force. He had a faraway, dismissive attitude as he strolled the terraces, which seemed to attract rather than repel customers, as if the goods he had to offer were scarce, desirable and hard to come by; as if, indeed, he cared very little whether he sold any of them or not. This method worked wonders, and his tray emptied faster than anyone else's.

It must have been Bertie's success that introduced the commission on sales method of payment, and this in its time led to my downfall. No one could outsell Bertie, and in due course his pre-eminence was rewarded by a secret offer of the organiser's job.

I accepted my defeat with grace. After all, I remained the Chairman of the Anti-Communist League and, as such, the superior of Bertie in an even more prestigious field, the illegal arena of political action.

The enemy there was no longer the German army, with its row upon row of domed steel helmets, and its feet kicking high in the arrogance of the goose-step; it was now the grinding tracks of the Soviet tanks which had advanced from Stalingrad, disgorging, in the stale aftermath of victory, a sinister fifth column of industrial subverters, dangerous at lathe and anvil. So we supposed.

After all, Karl Marx had said the revolution would start in England. The school might say what it will, but we were still in the forefront of insight, aware of the panzers advancing over the shop floor, even before the managers themselves could see them.

Ice-cream and politics were not the only fields in which Bertie and I collaborated. At a slightly later date we expanded our commercial interests into butcher's knives and glassware. Indeed, we became a small company, with printed business cards in a neat Roman script in the name of FINEWARE.

I still possess a small set of FINEWARE cards with my own name and initials in the bottom left-hand corner as the company's sales representative. One of these cards could be swiftly extracted from a wallet and placed with a trumping flourish upon the counter of any interested, though slightly sceptical, retailer who suspected that we might, in view of our age, and inexperience, represent some sort of hoax.

We were not a hoax. We were an active and, I think, even a profitable company. We bought and ran our own van, a mustard-coloured Ford, in the back of which our stock of cleavers or five-ounce optics would rattle and chink in dangerous proximity.

Neither Bertie nor I could drive, and this necessitated the extension of the original group – which, needless to say, also included John Bingham, a fascinated though partly sleeping partner during his convalescence – to embrace a lively, mechanically minded boy whose main interest was in the vehicle.

The van was purchased for £100, and upon the demise of FINEWARE sometime during my first year at Oxford, it passed finally and unreluctantly, with no coughing demur, into the driver's private possession.

We started our trading with the glassware, a range of pub and club stock which varied from half-dozens of pint tank-ards, gauged and massive, through so-called five-ounce Worthingtons with their wide-shouldered rims down to, or possibly up to, the rather fancy and rarely sold liqueur and spirit vessels, notably advocaat glasses, with their thin stems and pinched sides.

These were obtained at a wholesale rate from a huge man in a straw-filled room, and were offered for sale over a vague area that included Rotherham, Barnsley and Chesterfield, where I would sometimes pause for a delicious cream bun at a small baker's under the shadow of the church with the crooked spire.

Clubs were best, since their requirements were gargan-tuan, and their budgets lax enough to allow a well-disposed employee to give us a helping hand to the extent of a few dozen extra sherry glasses. Individual publicans were often suspicious, canny and even hostile, urging us not to butt in where others were already running the trade.

Nevertheless, a modest income was made. Enough, in fact, to encourage our diversifying into our second, and more suitably Sheffield, line: the retailing of butcher's knives.

I forget which enterprising firm of cutlers granted us access to the glitter of the meat world, but I remember the knives themselves very well, their dark, hafted handles, and their dulled, razor-sharp, sweeping blades.

John Bingham acquired a particular affection for these grim reminders of animal mortality, and his room at New College, a barren cavern of a place, was decorated with a jaunty spread on a clean linen napkin.

Sales of butcher's knives were always less brisk than those of glassware. Very few butchers would want to invest in more than one at a time, and the merchandise moved with a painful slowness.

We decided to branch out, abandoning the comparative safety of the support units, the butcher's shops. We approached the infantry in the front line, the slaughtermen themselves, in action inside the abattoirs.

I have sharp and messy memories of these slippery encounters. I recall once trying to keep my foothold on a slew of offal, still reeking from the slit belly, while a preoccupied man in a leather apron dispatched a series of squealing hogs with a captive-bolt gun in a low pen.

It was neither easy nor dignified to lean over a reeking pig version of Dante's inferno and attempt to attract a slaughterman's attention with a glossy, brand-new cleaver. Still, it was done sometimes, and with some success.

I have seen a man reach into his pocket with bloodstained fingers, and buy a knife from me then and there, employing its edge on the living skin within seconds of passing the greasy pound notes into my hand.

There can be no sentimentality in a meat-eating community. I disliked the evidence of pain and fear, and the immediacy of the transmission from life to death. All this was vividly present everywhere in the slaughterhouses. But I still enjoy pork, and I eat my chops and my bacon without feeling a sense of guilt, or a desire to vomit.

In the direct sale of butcher's knives, the war, so it seems to me now, had brought us at last within the wire, and had launched our adult careers on the killing-floor, marking our cheeks and wrists with spots of gore, and warning us of what the world would really be like — a place to survive in, where others would have to ache and die. It was a brutal lesson, but one I had started to learn when the sirens first blew in 1939.

22

The period beginning in September 1950 was to be an *annus mirabilis*. I had already tasted the sweets of power as a school prefect, with access to the private room at the right of the Assembly Hall, where the table-tennis table would sometimes be stripped of its net so that a drumhead court martial could be held, and some poor lad who had committed an offence such as talking at school lunch summarily sentenced and treated to a beating.

There were only two prefects senior to me that September, the Head Prefect and Captain of the soccer eleven, P. K. Fletcher, and the slightly crippled but still military Grade II John Bingham. Both were to leave at Christmas, called up for the army.

I myself had gone to my Conscription Board at the Public Library, knowing already what the outcome would be. Several men had died recently on route marches, and they were taking no chances on anyone with a weak heart. I went down as Grade IV as soon as they clapped their stethoscopes to my murmur, and I was back on the street with a green card, excused on medical grounds.

I didn't like this then, and I don't like it now. I have endless fantasies of enlisting in some guerrilla unit with low or no health standards and dying like Guevara in a remote jungle. I once even considered the French Foreign Legion and the Tunisian desert as properties for my euthanasia dream.

Most people, I imagine, would regard my escape as a fortunate and a perfectly honourable one. After all, even John Bingham, as mad about the army as I, discovered that military life in the Canal Zone could be less of an inspiring adventure than a vindictive routine.

It doesn't matter. I still regard a spell in the army in the spirit of a child forbidden to attend a party, who is told that he wouldn't have enjoyed it anyway, and that it wasn't the sort of affair he thought it would be.

As it happened, it was the avoidance of military service that led to my appointment as Head Prefect. There simply wasn't anyone else left, or no one as senior as I. So that in January 1951, some days before my nineteenth birthday, I stepped easily through the glass doors at morning assembly, pacing after the headmaster to my new place on the front row of benches, while the whole school stood to attention.

This kind of ritual honour, like reading the lesson at the end of term, the cynosure of all eyes behind the eagle, appealed to my sense of public ceremony. There has never since been such a sensation of authority exhibited as outward power.

There were responsibilities too. The right, for example, to preside at those grim-faced sessions of adolescent sadism when our juniors were judged and punished. I used to write out my prosecuting harangues in pencil, and deliver them like speeches for some Jacobean tragedy, quivering with right-eous denunciation.

I must have been a monster. I even improved the instruments of chastisement, admitting the introduction of a ridged galosh instead of the traditional gym shoe. The beatings record, as it was known, was broken in my second term.

One factor contributing to this opportunity was the arrival, only one term earlier, of a new and evidently more cautious headmaster, Nathaniel Clapton. He proved much too willing to accept a glib senior boy's interpretation of normal practice, and I made full use of this benefit.

There was a terrible hubris in all this. I would risk a combination of legal supremacy with underground intrigue, masquerading as the embodiment of law and order at school lunches, while riding in nightly gangsterism, like a distributor of bootleg liquor, on the nefarious business of the ACL.

Indeed, on one occasion, so far did the desire to make a mock of authority go that I collected all the toilet rolls from the Mount Hotel in Leeds, where three of us had been staying as candidates for a scholarship from the University, packed them up in a parcel, and then returned them through the post with a note saying that they came with the compliments of Nathaniel Clapton.

These pointless gestures and flexings of the muscles of

pride were, indeed, to precede a fall, though not, as it happened, a lapse from power. It was the soft inner core of the daemon, the tender heart of the strutting dictator, on which the gods had their eye.

They waited for their moment, and then they struck.

The blow fell in its own time. Even after I began to feel its pressures, though, the blessings of external success continued to shower down, as manna or confetti from heaven.

I had already been appointed Chairman of my youth club and, as such, had been entered by the adult club leader, the father of a school friend, called Dr Fells, for a travelling scholarship to the United States.

There were to be five of these scholarships, one reserved for a delegate of the body to which we were affiliated, the National Association of Girls' and Mixed Clubs. In the event, after a series of ever-tougher interviews, which increasingly tested a sordid ability to seem young Mr Nice Guy, I was fortunate enough to gull the London board, no doubt then partly sympathetic to my need for a change of scene, into seeing me as the right choice for their highly desirable post.

I was chosen to be what was laughingly called a youth ambassador, travelling, with four other boys, the length and breadth of the United States, boarding with rich WASP families, and being wined and dined, wooed and bewomened, as if we were princes of the British royal blood. One of us, a striking dark Adonis from Marlborough, perhaps was. The others came from more modest backgrounds, a Bob from the steel industry, and a Mick from the sugar one, and a particularly suave and slightly older Colin from the National Association of Boys' Clubs.

Inevitably, my own role led to some confusion on the other side of the Atlantic. Strapping jocks would stare in horror as they gazed at someone they had eagerly expected to be their ravishing English date, the dazzling belle from the National Association of Girls' and Mixed Clubs. How could she possibly be a boy?

He was, though, and he profited, in time, from the flood of female flesh as lavishly as his fellow-travellers. But all this was to come later, and after the blow had fallen, and the trauma taken hold.

America took me to her bosom, and I am grateful for it. I had never, save once, ever been abroad before, and that was only for two weeks to France, where John Bingham and I, picked up at Versailles by an elderly gay banker, were transported to Paris and there put up and platonically courted with French and food, ensconced, I am sure to the distinguished gentleman's prurient if vicarious delight, in an exiguous double truckle-bed.

Neither John Bingham nor my other best male friend Anthony Thwaite, is to any degree homosexual, but I have slept with both. Indeed, in the Thwaite case, a special mattress was stripped from its polythene cover by the proprietor of the Fantasy Press, in order that this cohabitation might be possible.

These collocations mark an age of innocence. Our generation was prone to call homosexuals queers or even bum-boys, and the coarseness of the language masked the crudity of the understanding. We were unaware of our attractiveness to our own sex, and I was deeply shocked, though also much amused, to be wooed along the banks of the Seine, when wearing an American army bush shirt which gave my chest a certain florid fullness, by a disgraceful man who inaugurated a conversation on the position of the human heart and, upon hearing me suggest that it was located somewhere in the breast, at once embarked upon a vivid ostensive definition, plunging his hand forward and down towards my kilt, saying, no doubt by way of correction, 'En France, Monsieur, le coeur c'est là.'

The kilt was admired in France, though, and the Auld Alliance worked its wonders. I was once about to be turned away from the Paris Opéra, deemed to be wearing short trousers, and then profusely apologised to, when the attendant observed that I was in fact garbed in the costume of my country, the swinging masculine colours of the 'ladies from Hell', who had fought side by side with the descendants of Napoleon's *grande armée* both in 1914 and 1939.

The kilt swayed, and it held me to home, and Scotland. I was photographed in the garden, beside the bending naked statue, my hand on my arm, and a dirk tucked into my stocking top, the pleats of the tartan falling in dark folds along my thigh.

I was ill with pride, sure of my destiny, and aware of the future as a ladder expanding on to infinity. What could occur to halt my advance to ever-higher rungs of achievement? Nothing, it seemed.

Nothing, except my mother's illness. When that came it burned the sweets of power to ashes in my mouth. It took its time, and it did it slowly, but there was no escape.

I ended my *annus mirabilis* in a trauma of grief.

23

My mother was ill for a long time. Longer than I realise, perhaps. I was too busy with my many concerns to know exactly what was the matter with her. She had always been so strong, and I was the invalid. It was hard to see things in reverse.

I know that she went into hospital for some days, and then came out, and seemed only a little better. But then I suppose I thought she was getting old, and old people were often slower, and more crotchety.

I helped as much as I could, or at least I thought I did. I would make my own tea, and sometimes my mother's too, even if this was no more than some toast, and a scone or two, and a pot of Brooke Bond blend. I went for the doctor if he was needed, and I accepted the fact that my mother wanted to spend more time in bed, or stretched out on the settee.

One time she had shingles, and I remember the terrible painfulness of the blisters at the base of her spine. But that got better. It wasn't shingles that was making her ill. Whatever was making her ill was giving her shingles.

Autumn of 1950 was a crisp season, and I wrote a long poem, describing Broomhill as a typical suburb, a derivative piece, and then I wrote a shorter poem in late October, about walking across the Botanical Gardens, and sloughing leaves, and missing my mother, and this was the best thing I'd ever written, although I didn't know it, and the only thing I wrote in my teens that remains in any way worth reading.

I watched my mother get worse. But I didn't really know she was getting worse. The photographs of her taken with Aunt Margaret in the garden show a greying woman with a slight stoop, and her hand in the pocket of a stylish jacket. They show a strained smile, too, when I look at them now, and my Aunt Margaret very grim. Perhaps she knew something, or guessed something, that I didn't know.

I don't remember very many details. But I do remember,

like the flash of a blade, the time I woke up in the middle of the night and heard my mother groaning aloud in the other room. By this time Miss Green was no longer living with us, and we were alone in the house.

I got up in my pyjamas and went through to find out what was the matter. But there was nothing to see, nothing to know. Just my mother in terrible pain. I asked if I ought to get the doctor, but she wouldn't let me. She just shook her head, and then something would shake her inside, and the sounds came out again.

I went back to bed, and I tried to sleep, and I couldn't. I'd seen my mother weak and ill before, but I'd never known her like this, unable, or so it seemed, to control her response to pain.

I don't know how long it lasted, or when I went for the doctor, but I don't think it made, in the end, a very great deal of difference. The ambulance came, and they took her away, the way they had taken me, too, only six years earlier, to the Royal Hospital. But there was one difference. I came back. My mother stayed away.

I wonder what she thought when she was carried out through the front door of 7 Southbourne Road for the last time? It wasn't much of a house, with its pebble-dash front, and its oblong bay windows, and its evergreen laurel bushes, and its rhubarb she used to make pies for me from. It wasn't even her own house, it was only rented still. But it had been her home.

A few months later the furniture went under the hammer in an auction room, or was given away to friends, or was disposed of, the better items, piecemeal to grasping dealers. The three-piece suite my mother and I had sat and talked in all our shared lives was transported, at my request, to the Stokes's, where it was well taken care of, for many more years.

The grandfather clock that had stood in the hall and been started whenever it stopped with a push of its great brass pendulum was taken away to the Stokes's, too, but most of the house was dismantled and sold.

The porcelain and the silver, the carpets and the piano, the chest of drawers that had once held my poems, and the Singer sewing-machine that had mended my torn trousers, the basket chair from the kitchen, and the set of studded Jacobean dining chairs, the things from the larder and the sheets from the beds, all were lifted and torn up as if by some invisible, slow wind, and scattered, as they had been eleven years earlier by the blast of the land-mine, but now more inexorably, in the aftermath of a life's climax, never to be reassembled, or known again, except in my own brain.

Even the octagonal wag clock, with its dangling chains, and its decorated face, which someone would know how to wind and make go, this, too, was taken from its place on the wall, and left its light shadow. But all this was later, months on in the summer.

In the meantime, my mother was taken away to hospital. She was put in a nice clean ward, and well taken care of. But no one knew how to wind the springs of her illness, or touch her decorated face, or push the brass pendulum, which had frozen to stiff stone in her liver.

Of course it was only a matter of time. But no one knew that then.

My mother was in hospital for several months. I don't know exactly what date it was when she went in, though I could check it easily enough from the five-year diary I used to keep. Somehow I don't want to know the detail, I simply want to recall the feel.

The feel is of sometime before Christmas, while I was involved in producing a one-act play for the youth club, a detective mystery in which I managed to combine the direction, Olivier-wise, with a performance of the leading role. It was another of my arrogances, the wish to be number one in everything.

I saw myself now, I suppose, as an active adult involved in a myriad various concerns, able and individual, visiting regularly an ill mother in hospital, someone who would be there for an indefinite period, and then be well, and come home.

My mother was only forty-seven, and although this undoubtedly seemed very old to me, it was not an age that I had ever had cause to associate with terminal illness. I inevitably assumed that she would in time get better. She might continue to ail, of course, and this, no doubt, would be an inconvenience, but I would be going away to Oxford, and I wouldn't be there to be bothered by it. The burden would have to be borne by someone else.

This kind of callousness must seem very shocking now, and indeed it was. But no one told me, if anyone knew, that my mother was going to die. For her to get better, and be an invalid, would be bad enough. But I was an invalid myself. I'd been one for six years. I knew just how bad it was, and how you could cope.

So I didn't worry about my mother. I went to see her, and I took her grapes and magazines, and I told her all the news of my busy life, or at least those parts of the news that were suitable for an adult and a mother to hear.

There was plenty to tell. I was in the thick of the Oxford examination period and made a visit down to Queen's to sit for a Hastings Scholarship. I didn't get one, and I had to return in January, suffering acute pain from a coming wisdom tooth, and sit for an Open Scholarship in Classics at New College, which I did get.

It was simply yet another in the series of blessings that were showering on me, as if I was an actor on a limelit stage and the gods were literally tossing bouquets of flowers down at my feet. But it gave my mother a lot of pleasure.

I see her sitting propped up on the pillows, wearing a blue cardigan that shows her strong forearms, and smiling at the thought of what her little son was going to do in the world, and how pleased his father would have been, if he could have lived to know.

Sometimes I think my father would have qualified his approval, preferring me to have won a scholarship in physics or chemistry, and gone on to be an engineer like himself, and make a great deal more money than I am ever likely to make out of pushing a pen.

But my mother was absolute in her joy. An achievement was an achievement, whatever the outcome or the consequences, and it ought to be admired. I basked in her smile, adding it to all the other tributes to my intellectual prowess, another bright feather amid the heaping trophies of ambition.

I never knew how precious, in retrospect, it would be.

For some months my mother's condition seems to have been stable. I knew now what her illness was said to be. It was described as cirrhosis of the liver. Even today, putting down this diagnosis, I recognise a reticence, knowing how this disease is almost always, in laymen's minds, associated with drinking.

Blindness about the vices of one's parents is a chronic thing, and there will be many who suppose that some merciful censor has excised all recollection of a last, shameful horror, when I say that I have no memory of my mother ever touching spirits, except in the process of mixing me a hot toddy – a glass of whisky and honey, sometimes to be swallowed with a butter ball – for a cold.

It is inconceivable to me that an alcoholic habit of sufficient dimensions to induce cirrhosis could have been sustained without my being aware either of empty bottles, or of intoxicated behaviour, or of unwashed glasses.

Then perhaps, I have told myself, years on, it was another thing, eating at the liver with the voracious appetite of that awe-inspiring scourge we designate by the sign of the crab. It would have fitted the muffling sympathy of my elders at the time to have thought to soften the pain by disguising the nature of my mother's illness.

But then, I knew nothing of cancer. It was more likely I would be worried, as I have been since, by the thought of cirrhosis. I come back, therefore, into mystery: the proper destination, I believe, for any inquiry into the reasons for the expiry of human consciousness.

I have no desire to inspect the doctor's records, or to question surviving friends. What took my mother away was a force too alien for any medical analysis, too oblique in its bearing for any Freudian or other interpretation.

In the panorama of decease, we confront the nightmare of the soul. Bare back it takes us, who knows where.

The crisis of my mother's illness came in April. Between the first of the snowdrops and the last of the daffodils, whatever was haunting the draughty attic of her spirits had worked through its visitation.

One afternoon, when I went to see her, she seemed in worse pain. The sheets were mounded up now in a sort of a low hillock, and below those sheets lay the terrible distension of her belly, where the flooded liver was failing to extract the body's waste fluids.

I was told by a doctor, later — choosing a homely image, as he no doubt thought — that her liver had gone hard, like pumice stone. I never brush my nails with a bath-sized piece now without remembering. The little rat's head, porous like a skull, seems to stiffen with evil reminiscence in my fingers.

I was told that my mother was worse, and that I might stay the night, if I wanted to. I think I could scarcely understand, even then. But the message was clear enough. You didn't get invited to sit up all night in a hospital just because you were missing your mother's company.

I stayed. I suppose Mrs Stokes was there, too. Perhaps my Aunt Margaret. I don't remember. Legend has wanted to strip them all away from the canvas, and leave me alone with my mother at the end. I don't think anyone else was important.

She breathed very heavily all night, and I sat there beside her, sleeping perhaps, or waking. I don't know. I know that I held her hand.

In the morning she could still speak quite normally. She even seemed a little better. She knew, of course, why I was there and why I hadn't left her, but she said that she didn't think she was going to die.

Nevertheless, she wanted to make her will, and I left her for a little while to go out into the air and the sun and up Glossop Road to a newsagent's, where I bought the simplest kind of will form. I took it back to the ward, and my mother wrote out what she wanted to do.

It wasn't a difficult will for her to write. She just wanted to leave everything to me. What she was leaving, though, wasn't only there on the paper now. It was gathering out of her dying body, and out of all she had been, and settling into the ends of my nerves, and for the rest of my life.

There must have been people there to witness the will, but I don't remember who they were. After the will was written, and sealed, and put into an envelope, my mother and I were alone together for a little while. Tears came into her eyes, the only tears I remember her shedding, and they were tears of joy, not sadness. She squeezed my hand, and she said, and these are the last words I remember her saying:

'I've been so proud of you.'

Nothing that had happened before, or that has happened since, or will happen later, could ever live up to that faith, or that pride. I don't think I could find any way of answering what she said, or, if I did, I only shook my head, or squeezed her hand in return. I must have been far out in the sea of my own tears and, alas, they were not tears of joy, like hers.

They were tears of guilt.

In the afternoon, about four o'clock, I think, my mother died. Her breath came out of her mouth in a last slither, as if the serpent were leaving her, and she was ready for heaven. There is a death rattle. But it isn't a rattle.

I sat for a long time, just holding her hand, and looking at her face. It seemed very beautiful. Someone had come to see her with a bunch of spring flowers, and they were brought to the bedside by a nurse. I put them across her body, iris and daffodils. She would have liked them, but they came just too late for her to see.

Many years later, I wrote a poem about my father returning to stand at the head of my bed as I was dying of heart disease in old age. I like to think that he came that day in the uniform of a young soldier when my mother was dying, marvelling at how she was unchanged, though eleven years older. But perhaps he didn't come. Perhaps, like me, he found it unbearable to see her die.

Perhaps she wouldn't have wanted him to come. She would have wanted to spare him the sight of her suffering. But he would have come, if she had asked. He would have come, if he could.

Later, I emptied out my mother's bedside cupboard, and took home her crocodile handbag, and a little green bowl with a curling lip that she'd had for flowers. I went into her bedroom at Southbourne Road, and opened the first long drawer down in her chest of drawers.

I knew what she kept there. It was a long, crumpled white envelope, folded over at one end. Inside it there was a khaki lanyard, and the things my father had had in his pockets when he was killed. I put the little bowl and the crocodile handbag in beside them.

Since then, those things have been in many drawers, and once, when I had to move, in a cardboard box. But they have always been together. They lie now in the same room as my wife and I, when we go to sleep.

I like to think that my parents know, if through things they can know, that their son remembers, and that he is happy, as they would want him to be. When my own son was born I put these things in his cradle, and let his fingers touch them. He was too young to know what they were, but one day he will be older, and will understand.

One day these things will be his, the only bridge between the generations that never met, the best I can build.

That evening, back at home, I tried to put my thoughts in order. I was reading the last chapter of *A Farewell to Arms*, and I found solace, of a kind, in what Lieutenant Henry thinks, as he looks for the last time at the dead nurse he has loved.

'It was like saying goodbye to a statue.' For me it was the beauty of the statue rather than its inanimate material that struck home, and helped. I made up a bad Shakespearean line of poetry, trying to provide an epitaph for my mother, and then I wrote a long, muddled, rather George Barkerish poem called 'The Terminus' which was later printed in the school magazine.

But nothing much helped, really. On Sunday I went to Church, and much embarrassed the elders, one of whom told me later privately that, although they respected my bravery in coming to the service, it was normal for the relatives of the deceased to stay away one Sunday, so that the minister could avoid inflicting any inadvertent pain — or, I remember thinking grimly to myself, incurring any action for libel — in his valedictory prayer.

In time there was the funeral, and there were letters of sympathy, to be read and replied to. I was good at that. There was getting on with my own life, too, wearing my belted raincoat and my close-fitting pigskin gloves with their clasping orange buttons, the subjects of a poem themselves, and my pride and joy these months in their elegant, military neatness.

I saw myself as a commissioned soldier now, the survivor of a final trauma, where the unit had been obliterated, and the flag was still to be carried forward, always forward, across an open plain raked by the machine-gun fire of grief where there was no destination, no other side, other than the desperate, unpassable tangle of the enemy's wire, the aura of death. There one day, I would fall, too, handing on the flag to my own son. And so on, out through time.

The military metaphors have survived, inane and yet solacing. I remain a child of the war, seeing life as Edmund Wilson once said that Hemingway saw it, as through an arrow slit. This may be a bitter and a narrow view, but it gives a focus.

24

One of the defining parameters of my adult life has been short-sightedness. I discovered that I needed spectacles entirely by accident, at the age of twelve, when an optical test revealed that almost all of the burden of vision was being carried by my left, or sinister, eye.

In accordance with the prevailing ophthalmic wisdom, I was prescribed a pair of lenses calculated to spread the strain more evenly, in effect by weakening my good eye until I could no longer see perfectly clearly, but required the perpetual aid of glasses.

I now peer owlishly out at the world, through my arrow-slit, from behind a pair of rather limpidly athletic spectacles, aping, I would like to suppose, the sort of anti-dazzle pale-blue lenses affected by competition skiers, as the earlier lenses I was prescribed by the National Health mimed the round visionary aids of great Victorian preachers.

The result is the same, a clear view of a world which is in reality, for me, a Renoirish blur. I have never enjoyed Impressionism, no doubt for this very reason. My favoured art is the myopic exactness of Dali or the Pre-Raphaelites. Indeed, the landscape of atrocious confusion which looms forward whenever I take off my spectacles, whether to lapse into sleep or to wipe away tears, inevitably seems to be soothed by the clarity of representation which ground lenses invent.

Reality, in all its blurry sadness, is a shared experience. The great sea of grief washes at the shores of all our eyes. No one has privileged access to it. There is a line in Kafka, used by Anne Sexton as an epigraph for one of her collections of poems, about a good book being an axe for the sea frozen within us.

One's individual grief can seem to be a drop in the ocean, a single stalactite hung on the lip of an eave. But this pinnacle of ice may melt in a thaw of sympathy, and may even fall, and touch some fellow-creature to the heart.

Sadness can hurt, even as it communicates. But it can also inspire. As in a chandelier, its constituent parts, ranged like fragments of crystal, in tiers of tears, can reflect a brilliant, undying light into the darkest corners of our lives.

It isn't, though, any private authority of the grief that matters. This is the fallacy of those who admire their own sadness too much. One life is much like another. What matters is the shape and pattern provided by the chandelier-maker. The light comes from the form, not the substance.

There is a wonderful line in Vaughan, about seeing Eternity the other night, like a great ring of pure and endless light, all calm as it was bright. The calm, perhaps, is as important as the brilliance.

Those who have suffered from a migraine will know that it is often accompanied by the gradual approach of a flickering semi-circle of dazzling light, the arc of an internal neon light in the ballroom of the retina. But for them it is more like the ring of flames in the fire-storm when the bombs obliterated the city of Dresden.

Through some mercy of the powers of light, I have often enjoyed this phenomenon without the concomitant agony of the headache. I see a small, prismatic, quartz-like letter C, like the filament inside a light-bulb approaching from the mid-point of my field of vision.

As it comes closer, it seems to move higher up until it covers the ceiling of my skull, glittering there like a hovering flamboyance of concentric rings, a spaceship of the brain.

This, I believe, is the concentrated ikon of a life drenched in its own grief, and attempting its miniature, and here private, sublimation. This is my chandelier of tears.

Every time the lights come, they remind me of sadness. Every time they go, they return me to laughter, and joy. But they return me with an after-echo of radiance, a luminous glow like a glimmer through a curtain drawn against the black-out, holding the raiders at bay.